Research Projects for College Students

Research Projects for College Students

WHAT TO WRITE ACROSS THE CURRICULUM

Marilyn Lutzker

Greenwood Press

New York
Westport, Connecticut
London

Library of Congress Cataloging-in-Publication Data

Lutzker, Marilyn.
  Research projects for college students : what to write across the
curriculum / Marilyn Lutzker.
    p.   cm.
  Bibliography: p.
  Includes indexes.
  ISBN 0-313-25149-5 (lib. bdg. : alk. paper)
  1. Report writing. 2. Research. 3. Interdisciplinary approach in
education. I. Title.
LB2369.L83   1988
808'.02—dc19   87-37549

British Library Cataloguing in Publication Data is available.

Library of Congress Catalog Card Number: 87-37549
ISBN: 0-313-25149-5

First published in 1988

Greenwood Press, Inc.
88 Post Road West, Westport, Connecticut 06881

Printed in the United States of America

The paper used in this book complies with the
Permanent Paper Standard issued by the National
Information Standards Organization (Z39.48-1984).

10 9 8 7 6 5 4 3 2 1

Contents

Appendices

Acknowledgments

To my friends, and to my colleagues in the library of John Jay College
of Criminal Justice, I offer thanks for their help and support, and apol-
ogies for my demands on their time and patience. Many ideas offered
by friends and colleagues have been incorporated into this book. William Coleman, Karen Kaplowitz, Patricia Licklider, Shirley Schnitzer,
and Marne Tabb, all of the English Department at John Jay, have
knowingly or unknowingly, made their contributions. For their will-
ingness to read and criticize the entire book and discuss and share their
own ideas, I would like to thank Luther Carpenter, Eleanor Ferrall,
Olive James, and Jack Lowenherz. A special acknowledgment is made
to Eileen Rowland and Wanda Evans, who have both been particularly
giving of time, effort, and support.

Introduction

This book, written by a college librarian, is addressed to college teachers in all disciplines. Its goal is to increase the satisfaction of both student and teacher with undergraduate research/writing projects.

WHY SUCH A BOOK FROM A LIBRARIAN?

The Writing Across the Curriculum movement began, and is spreading among colleges and universities, because of a growing awareness that most students do not write well. The leaders of the movement have shown that if students are to learn to write well, they must write often—which means incorporating writing into every course in the curriculum. There are many ways to do this. This book is concerned with only one of them: designing writing assignments that are directly tied to library-based research.

Although the vision of the college library as the heart of the academic institution may no longer be apt (if indeed it was ever more than an idealization), the library remains one of the few places frequented by students at every level and faculty from every discipline. Librarians thus have a unique perspective from which to observe what is happening in the academic program of the whole school, not simply in one department or another. The reference librarian in particular often feels like a central switching station for students' research assignments. From this central position at the reference desk, librarians see how often boredom and frustration on the part of both faculty and students negate the potential value of research/writing projects.

We too are frustrated. We sit surrounded by treasures in print and microform; we have carefully selected for our collection works that will not only give students the information they know they need, but works we hope will challenge them to explore worlds they haven't yet thought about. We are proud of the resources available to our students and frustrated when they are not used.

This book is a compilation of ideas aimed at transforming frustration into challenge. Some of the ideas (there are no prescriptions) are mine. Most, however, have come from conversations with faculty and friends at my own college and elsewhere, and from readings in the library literature and the literature of other disciplines. I have tried to give credit where appropriate, but ideas are often not easily traceable, for which I ask scholarly forgiveness.

I don't anticipate that many will use these ideas exactly as they are presented; curriculum, students, and faculty are too varied for that. Rather, I offer them as starting points for designing individualized projects to meet specific needs. A word of caution: since these are ideas and suggestions, not preplanned and predigested "lesson plans," they may require a good deal of active planning on the part of the teacher who uses them.

There are three basic themes explored in this book:

1. Research assignments that are both intellectually meaningful and pedagogically useful can be difficult to design. Chapters 1, 2, and 3 present suggestions for handling these difficulties.

Chapter 1 analyzes the underlying objectives of most research/writing assignments and discusses the relationship between content objectives and writing and research skills. Chapter 2 offers suggestions for selecting and assigning topics and structuring assignments. Chapter 3 discusses some potentially useful library services and offers a compendium of tips on how to work with the library staff to best achieve your objectives. Chapter 4 is a recognition that the procedures and forms of scholarly documentation are a necessary part of academic research, even for the undergraduate. It suggests ways to help students grasp the intellectual concepts that underlie the forms of scholarly documentation.

2. Variations in the format in which research findings are reported can sometimes provide a more focused medium for the practice of certain research and writing skills than the traditional research paper. Such

alternative formats may stimulate enthusiasm from students who have previously had negative experiences with term papers. Many of these alternate formats, discussed in Chapter 5, are either for very short projects, or are adaptable to projects of varying lengths.

3. Through imaginative exploitation of library resources, instructors can design research/writing projects that will interest both the student researcher and the faculty audience and that will achieve the goals of the assignment.

How can the wonderful resources in our libraries be used to vary and enrich undergraduate research experiences? In some instances, simply by introducing undergraduates to sources usually reserved for "real scholars"; in others by taking a new approach to the materials traditionally used by undergraduates. I pay particular attention to primary sources because they are so often underutilized in undergraduate research assignments and because it is only in recent years that so many of them have become widely available. The selection of sources to be discussed in Part III, although based on estimates of general interest and availability, reflects personal choice and represents only a few of the thousands available. These resources are discussed in Chapters 6, 7, 8, 9, and 10.

Use of the kinds of materials discussed in these chapters will virtually guarantee that the work submitted will not be the output of a term-paper mill, or another student's recycled paper.

PART I

Objectives for Research Assignments

The assignment of research papers to undergraduates is traditional; so too are complaints from students about the process, and from faculty about the product. Despite occasional demurrers in the literature, the need for research papers is widely accepted and the reason for assigning them is rarely questioned.[1]

If many instructors have a secret reason for assigning term papers it is perhaps the hope that their students will experience the satisfaction that comes from discovering new ideas, and the exhilaration that comes from sleuthing in the sources and locating missing data. They hope that students will discover that sifting through information and ideas and organizing them into a coherent statement, although difficult and often frustrating, can, in the end, be a rewarding experience. Most scholars and librarians have experienced these feelings; to have our students know them also should, perhaps, be the primary objective of all term-paper assignments.

The stated reasons for such assignments usually fall into three areas: to master content, to improve writing skills, and to develop library research skills. Critical thinking, sometimes considered a separate skill, is always an objective in research-paper assignments and is integrally related to the other three objectives. This chapter suggests ways in which the skills objectives, particularly the research skills objectives, can be integrated most efficiently with the content objectives of the assignment.

CONTENT OBJECTIVES

The mastery of specific facts, theories, and ideas is the prime objective of most research/writing assignments, except perhaps for those in composition and research methods classes. Many writing assignments require students to go to the library, but do not require library research skills and can not be considered true research papers. Often students can meet the content objectives of a paper by selecting titles from a bibliography prepared by the instructor, or, more often, by reading materials placed on library reserve. Confusion and misunderstanding can result, however, if the result of this kind of assignment is called a library research paper. Students must understand that using the reserve room does not constitute a library research skill and that looking up prescribed titles in the library catalog constitutes only the lowest level of library skill.

An example follows of three different approaches to combining a content objective with the use of the library. The class has read *All Quiet on the Western Front*, and the basic content objective is to increase the students' understanding of the novel.

In the first approach, there is no concern with furthering library research skills. The instructor puts the most appropriate critical works on library reserve, and the students are required to read them.

In the second approach, a determination to have the students learn the basic library procedures for locating literary criticism is added to the desire to have them better understand the novel.

The method is to require that students themselves locate relevant critical material in several journal articles. While perhaps not meeting all content objectives (material the students uncover may not contain all the information the instructor would like them to have about the novel), this method will teach students how to use the *Essay and General Literature Index*, the *MLA Bibliography*, and the library's periodicals holding list. Moreover, the assignment may give students their first try at locating information in scholarly journals. This research assignment can be supplemented with the reading of prescribed materials held on library reserve, to provide a common basis for class discussion.

A third way to use the library to increase students' understanding of the novel would concentrate on recreating the historical context of the book. This is an alternate approach to library skills objectives for instructors who feel that research in nonliterary sources would be more appropriate or more interesting for their students. The students could be asked first to use the *New York Times Index* to locate first-hand descriptions of the battles described in the novel. The assignment could be further expanded to include the use of encyclopedias and biographical dictionaries for background information, and a variety of periodical indexes to locate both contemporary descriptions and later historical studies of the events.

RESEARCH SKILLS OBJECTIVES

Most undergraduates need to learn that efficient and effective research is a coherent logical process, requiring organization, planning, and evaluation. It is possible to acquire enough information for a reasonably acceptable paper by serendipitously roaming through the library, or by assembling facts from a textbook, three copies of a newsmagazine found at home, and two library books borrowed from a friend. Such papers may meet the content objectives of the assignment without having taught the student anything about using the library. The instructor establishes some control over the content objectives of a paper by judging the end result; control over the library research objectives is best achieved by controlling the process.

Although effective library research as an overall process needs to be taught from an overall, or holistic, point of view, individual research skills are relatively simple to isolate and to teach. While the ultimate hope is that students will learn to work efficiently with all kinds of library resources, academically acceptable research projects can be designed that utilize only a limited number of research skills.

The key questions in designing such assignments are: What is the relationship between the content and research objectives? and What is their relationship to the topics under consideration?

A brief and fairly obvious list of specific library skills follows. The instruction librarian or reference librarian can expand the list and help determine those skills most appropriate for your students, your library, and your content objectives.

- Know what is included in the library catalog; if the library has more than one catalog, as most do today, know the limitations of each.
- Be able to use the catalog efficiently. In many schools today, this involves a knowledge of key word searching, Boolean operators, and stop words, in addition to the traditional author, title, and subject approaches. The library catalog has always been a complex tool, and is more so today. The great danger is that it appears simple, and can almost always yield some results. Students must

realize that although the simple result may appear adequate, it is not always the best; the approach that worked to locate a book about the causes of crime may not be the best approach to locating a book about a famous murderer.

- Know the appropriate indexing or abstracting services for the subject. In a few instances the *Readers' Guide* (which is what students think of as a periodical index) is the best way to locate articles, but in many others, sources like *Historical Abstracts, Criminal Justice Periodical Index,* or *Psychological Abstracts* would be better.

- Locate relevant citations using the appropriate indexes.

- Be able to ascertain if your library owns the journal needed, what format it is in, and where it is located.

- Know how to obtain books and journal articles that are not in the home library.

- Know the function of tools such as *Bibliography Index, Essay and General Literature Index, Social Science Citation Index,* and *Index to Proceedings in the Humanities,* where they are appropriate.

- Know what newspapers are available in the library and how to use the available newspaper indexes.

- Know how to locate, evaluate, and use printed bibliographies and literature reviews.

- Know how to locate and evaluate relevant statistics.

- Know how to locate government documents, using such tools as the *CIS/Index* and the *Monthly Catalog.*

- Know how to locate and use subject encyclopedias and handbooks in order to get overviews of the field.

- Know how to locate biographical information and names and addresses.

- Know the important reference books in a specific subject area.

- Understand the concepts of computerized bibliographic searching and know about its availability on the campus.

- Be able to evaluate sources.

Students learn to "do research" when they learn about the existence of tools and procedures and how to use them effectively. If one objective of the assignment is to encourage students to learn specific tools and procedures, then successful completion of the assignment must require that those tools and procedures be used. The following are some suggested ways to integrate the use of specific tools into an assignment.

- In a discipline in which journals are important the assignment could specify that the bibliography include X number of articles.

- If the objective is to have the student locate those citations in an organized fashion rather than by just browsing, then the assignment can specify that five years of a specific index or indexes be searched and all relevant citations listed (not necessarily read).

- If knowledge of statistical sources is important, the assignment can specify that arguments be buttressed by statistics located in a statistical source and not those accompanying the textual matter.

- If an understanding of the difference between popular literature and scholarly literature is important, examples of each can be required to be properly labeled.

- If government documents are important in the subject area, the assignment can specify that at least one such source be used.

Additional suggestions are given in Chapter 2.

WRITING SKILLS

A full discussion of the theories and methods of teaching writing skills is not within the scope of this book. But because writing is necessary to communicate research findings, and because writing is intimately related to thinking, it is virtually impossible to divorce writing skills from content and research objectives.

Writing skills required to meet content objectives range from those needed for a one-page summary of a chapter in a textbook to those needed for an organized, documented, analytical research paper that draws upon a large body of primary and secondary sources and fills twenty pages. Whatever the size or format, the goal is a paper in which sound information is logically organized and properly presented. For that, students must have a grasp of at least rudimentary principles of composition and diction; a mastery of the mechanics of grammar, punctuation, and spelling; and the ability to locate, analyze, and organize information.

The literature on writing skills is clear about the efficacy of frequent writing followed by immediate feedback and required revision for improving student writing. There is also considerable agreement on the advantages of frequent short assignments, and of incremental projects that allow for feedback during the preparation of a long paper. The emphasis in this book is on research projects designed to take advantage of these findings.

CLARIFYING THE OBJECTIVES FOR THE STUDENT

No matter how simple or complex the objectives of the assignment may be, students need to understand them and recognize them as reasonable and important. Students who understand the relationship between clear thinking and clear writing, and who are aware that both are among the objectives of the assignment, are more likely to spend the extra time needed on the organization, grammar, and mechanics of presentation. Similarly, students are less likely to begrudge the time needed for organized and effective research if they know that the acquisition of research skills is one objective of the assignment, and if they understand why they are expected to learn those skills.

Students have a right to know what to expect. If the teacher provides a written assignment that includes the objectives, the scope, and, where appropriate, the specific tools and processes to be used, the students will have a clear reference point. A copy of the statement sent to the library will help the staff anticipate and understand the students' needs.

NOTE

1. Many books and articles discuss the rationale for term papers. Among the most helpful from the point of view of library research are: Faber, "Alternatives to the Term Paper," Ford and Perry, "Research Paper Instruction in the Undergraduate Writing Program," Griffin, "Using Writing to Teach Many Disciplines," Larson, "Research Paper in the Writing Course: A Nonform of Writing," Schwegler and Shamoon, "The Aims and Process of the Research Paper." *See also* Ford, Rees, and Ward, "Research Paper Instruction: A Comprehensive Bibliography, 1923-1980."

2

Structuring the Assignment and Choosing the Topic

STRUCTURING THE ASSIGNMENT

Today most educators recognize that it is during the process of researching and writing a paper that learning takes place; the final product is at best a report of that learning. There is also increasing recognition that more will be learned if the teacher can monitor and review what happens during the process, in addition to evaluating and grading the final result.[1]

As used here, the term *structured assignment* means an assignment composed of a number of small, interrelated projects done sequentially and culminating in a larger product. Such an assignment is valuable because:

- it permits multiple deadlines, so that all the work will not be left for the end;
- it permits early and frequent feedback, so that gaps in writing and research skills can be identified early;
- it provides "thinking time" between stages; and
- it takes advantage of the recognized efficacy of incremental learning.

A structured assignment does not ensure that students will enjoy the work any more than if they left it till the last minute, nor does it ensure that the final result will be any better than a last-minute product, but it makes both outcomes more likely.

One of the most anguished complaints of people marking under-graduate papers is that so few students seem able to grasp distinctions among the various modes of academic writing. Types of writing (actually types of thinking) that students are often required to distinguish among include: analysis, classification, comparison, contrast, criticism, definition, evaluation, paraphrasing, illustrating, justifying, reviewing, and summarizing. Mastery of these distinctions can be crucial for academic success; controlled practice with the opportunity for maximum feedback is one way to help students achieve this mastery.[2]

Instructors can build opportunities for practice in several of these types of writing into the research process early enough to contribute to the success of the final product. Not every piece of writing needs to be marked or graded; examples can be read and discussed in class, or students can assess each other's work.

In making assignments that incorporate these suggestions instructors should remind students of the long-range as well as short-range objectives of the assignment. Given students' grounding in traditional product/grade concepts, they may also need to be reassured that each piece of writing is not a separate entity, and to be encouraged to reuse or rework entire sentences and paragraphs from previously submitted segments.

At the same time that the importance of revision is being stressed, instructors can urge students who have not yet mastered word processing to take advantage of any services and facilities the school offers in this area. Most schools today have at the minimum some kind of open computer lab and on-line tutorials for word processing.

The following is a list of procedures that might be built into project designs to facilitate learning, monitor progress, and maximize opportunities for feedback. The nature of the assignment and the ability and previous experience of the students will determine a suitable selection.

- After explaining the scope, objectives, and procedures for the assignment, ask students to summarize in their own words what is expected. They can then compare their summaries with the written description you provide.

- Ask students to locate and read at least two encyclopedia articles for overviews of the subject, and to write a short summary of the articles. At least one of the articles should come from a subject encyclopedia. (Students will know about these from the library instruction session discussed in Chapter 3.)

- Be precise about the categories of materials to be used in the research and about the specific procedures to be used to locate them. (See list of suggested library skills objectives in Chapter 1.)

- Require a preliminary bibliography with a paragraph discussing the amount of material apparently available on the topic. This could also include a preliminary assessment of the value of certain types of material, or of specific items.

- Ask students to read two items on the bibliography that seem most promising for the final presentation, and then to analyze and compare them. Those who are still having difficulty differentiating between summarizing and analyzing might find it useful to summarize the articles first, and then analyze them. It is helpful if the items represent different points of view or different approaches; the items to be read can be selected by the student, or suggested by the teacher based on the preliminary bibliography.

- Alternatively, everyone in the class can read the same items, with some students asked to summarize, some to analyze, some to compare, some to outline, and some to evaluate. The results can be discussed in class; the best examples of each might be distributed for study.

- Where appropriate, an additional bibliography of sources for relevant statistics, primary sources, biographies, and government documents can be requested.

- Require a preliminary outline based on the initial reading. It might be very helpful to ask that this outline include a list of questions to be answered by further research, plus personal questions and doubts about the next research step, the organization, and the general tone to be adopted—in short, the kinds of questions students generally moan and groan about to their peers.

- Require a revised outline with one-paragraph summaries of what will be presented in each section. This outline should be more detailed than the preceding one.

- Request that students keep two sets of notecards for each item read (different colors are helpful). One set should contain a summary of the facts and opinions in the article; the other should contain analyses or evaluations of the information. Check the notecards until it is clear that students understand the difference between summary and analysis.

- Request a preliminary draft; it will reveal, and help students correct, any problems in organization and writing as well as gaps in the information. Asking students to return the draft, with your comments, along with the final paper will help you determine the extent to which corrections have been made.

- As an alternative to a required preliminary draft, students can be told that such drafts will accepted and corrected up to one week before the final paper is due.

USE OF WORKSHEETS AND RESEARCH LOGS

Research worksheets and evaluation forms can be used to provide structure for the inexperienced undergraduate researcher. The worksheet, by providing a framework for the recording of steps in the research process, can help to systematize and organize that process. The evaluation form, by providing a framework for the analysis of the works read, can help to stimulate a more analytical reading style. Examples of both types of forms are reproduced in Appendix D.

While the use of worksheets might be most appropriate for the less-   ·
prepared student, a personal research log will benefit students on all levels. Such a log is probably best when it is most informal. It should be used to record thoughts about the research process as well as steps actually undertaken and all sources consulted, whether helpful or not.

If students know they will be given credit for using reasonable sources even when the source does not yield the expected information, they may be encouraged to expand their research strategies. Crediting such efforts may also help dispel the feeling that a bibliographic "miss" has been a waste of time. The research log—like the worksheet—provides a means of offering credit for knowledge of bibliographic tools and for time spent with them; thus it encourages students to spend more time on the research process. In consequence, many will learn that more time spent in initial digging can yield more appropriate sources and hence a better end product. A research log can also give the instructor valuable insight into the student's way of thinking and working.

In addition to the other advantages of research worksheets and logs, the use of either is a virtual guarantee that the paper submitted will be the student's own work.

CHOOSING THE TOPIC

No matter what the objectives of the assignment, they can only be met within the context of the topic addressed. For many students the choice of a topic is the most difficult part of a research assignment. Academic librarians, frequently consulted by students desperately seeking a topic, can attest to their distress. We see them devoting hours to making what may ultimately turn out to be a poor decision, because library resources are either overwhelming or inadequate, the topic is too broad or too narrow, or the level of research needed is too complex. In all such cases, time is consumed in unproductive work, increasing the students' frustration without in any way contributing to their knowledge or skills.

Many instructors, recognizing the importance of motivation to successful research writing, invite students to write about "anything that really interests you," or "anything related to the course," in the hope that freedom of choice will stimulate greater interest in the project.

This approach, possibly a reflection of the efforts of the 1960s to make education "relevant," brings its own problems. The attempt to motivate by offering a free choice actually represents only the illusion of freedom of choice. Students can choose only from among those things they know; most undergraduates, particularly freshmen and sophomores, are fairly limited in both experience and knowledge. Despite some modest exposure to world history and American history, they frequently have little sense of the relationship of today's problems to those of the past, and what they know of today's problems is often limited to what occupies the most time and space in the media.

Thus, given free rein, students will choose from among a relatively small range of topics, which are, not surprisingly, the same topics that occupied their minds the year before when they were in high school. Librarians and teachers across the country will attest that complete freedom of choice in subject areas ranging from English composition to philosophy has resulted in hundreds of thousands of papers on abortion, capital punishment, and drug abuse, with child abuse, gun control, alcoholism, and AIDS as close followers.

These are obviously important subjects, but they have problems as topics for undergraduate research. Even assuming a student's continued interest in the subject, the research and writing process is unlikely to provide much intellectual stimulation. Novice researchers will have a hard time finding any significant arguments or insights that they have not already encountered. Furthermore, it is likely that some of the papers turned in will either belong to another student, have been written by the same student for another class, or will be the result of a "term paper mill." Finally, the boredom of the teacher who must read and grade one more paper on these time-worn topics is probably beyond description.

Students would be better served by being offered a controlled list of topics from which to select. To offer "anything you want to write about" as an assignment is like offering Pandora's box; it sounds enticing but presents problems. The person in control—the one who has set the objectives—is the one best able to ensure that topic and objectives are not in conflict, and to establish topics that will enable students to meet the objectives most successfully.

Assigning Topics in Skills Courses

Research assignments in skills-oriented classes offer students the opportunity to learn something entirely new. To deny them this opportunity in the belief that they will only enjoy working on topics immediately perceived as "relevant" is to miss a chance to broaden their knowledge and enlarge their horizons. Furthermore, these are the very classes in which free choice is least likely to yield a challenging, thought-provoking topic and most likely to produce work that is not entirely original.

There are thousands of effective research projects for these groups; many are suggested throughout this book. Lists of topics given to students should be annotated to pique interest, facilitate choice, and provide a reasonable departure for research.

Assigning Topics in Subject Courses

In a subject class, assignments will flow from the content of the course. Even here, students stand to benefit from a list of suggested topics drawn from the knowledge and experience of the instructor. Those who know the most about a subject know the best questions to ask.

Here too, annotating the topic list can awaken interest in unfamiliar areas and stimulate research into topics really new to the student. Annotations are particularly useful for topics that will be covered late in the semester.

A DIFFERENT APPROACH TO SELECTING TOPICS

Traditionally, after an area of inquiry is selected, the student, with or without help from the instructor or the librarian, will attempt to locate the best sources to use for the paper. There is an alternative approach. The instructor or librarian can first select sources that are potentially stimulating and exciting for students to use and then design topics based on those sources. This may sound artificial, but student research papers are artificial in terms of scholarly intent. They are, after all, exercises we devise to help students learn the nature of the scholarly enterprise, and we should design those exercises in the ways that best achieve the goal.

Part III of this book will be helpful to instructors wanting to attempt this approach. It discusses many nontraditional sources for undergraduate research, all of which can yield potentially exciting and challenging topics.

NOTES

1. Structured assignments are discussed in Griffin, "Using Writing to Teach Many Disciplines," Lefevre and Dickerson, *Until I See What I Say*, McCartney, "The Cumulative Research Paper."

2. Lefevre and Dickerson, *Until I See What I Say*, p. 52.

3

The Library Connection

WORKING WITH THE LIBRARIANS

Working with faculty to help student researchers is an important part of what librarians do. We take this responsibility seriously. However, we are real people working in a real (and usually underfunded and overly bureaucratic) environment. Like others in the academic community we often have more work to do than we can even conceive of finishing. Therefore, expect your library to help, but make an effort to learn something about the administration and organization of the library so that you can direct requests to the most appropriate person; involve the library in your planning as early as possible; and don't expect instant service, particularly on time-consuming tasks. Librarians are the most knowledgeable people on campus about what is available in the library (and other libraries as well), how to locate needed resources and information, and how to teach students to use the library.

The library staff can help teaching faculty improve student research projects in three major areas: initial planning of the project, teaching students how to do library research, and obtaining needed materials not available in the home library.

THE PLANNING PROCESS

Conferring with the library staff in the initial stages of planning a student research project offers many advantages. It will enable the librarian to suggest relevant materials in the collection and search out needed resources not in the collection. It can help make materials available by recalling titles out on loan, putting high-demand resources on reserve, and making certain that a needed index will not be sent to the bindery. In addition, the reference librarians will be better able to assist students if they have been alerted to the assignment, its objectives, and the expected level of research.

LIBRARY INSTRUCTION

Widespread recognition that library research is a complex process that students cannot be expected to learn on their own has led to increased acceptance of the idea of formal instruction in library procedures. Twenty years ago colleges that routinely offered such instruction were unusual; today it is a rare college that doesn't.

Library instruction programs in today's colleges can take one or more of a variety of forms:

- Printed, computer-assisted, or audio-visual guides. These range in size from short guides on how to use specific tools (for example, *Psychological Abstracts*) to bibliographies designed to help in locating specific kinds of information such as statistics or biographies to self-instructional workbooks on how to use the library.

- Conceptual, holistic discussions of information theory and of research strategies, methods, and tools. These can range from one-hour presentations to incoming freshmen to a full-semester class in research methods.

- Course-specific instruction—one or more sessions taught to enable students to meet the objectives of a particular assignment.

A course-related instruction session is the most efficient way to help students meet the research objectives of a specific assignment. Such a session enables the librarian to give an organized presentation of all the necessary material to the entire class. This is obviously preferable to having the reference librarians devote five or ten minutes each to those students who bother to stop at the reference desk.

Effective course-related library instruction requires close cooperation between teacher and librarian in the early planning stages. This will ensure that assignment objectives match available resources and the research skills and experience of the students. The way such sessions are scheduled and the amount of prior notice required vary, but more time is always better. Since the timing of the instruction session relative to the course outline is crucial, it is important to submit your request before the most appropriate time has been preempted. Normally, the classroom instructor—the link between the students, the assignment, and the library—is expected to be present and to participate in the presentation.

Many formats and instructional aids may be used in course-related library instruction: lectures, discussions, slides or transparencies to reinforce the content of the lecture or discussion, hands-on work with the materials, tours of the relevant sections of the library, brief in-class exercises, workbooks or worksheets to be done after class, printed bibliographies, and sample explanatory pages. Some libraries routinely include in their instruction program discussions of topic selection, note taking, outlining, and documentation; others limit themselves to instruction in research tools and strategies.

As mentioned earlier, either in conjunction with teaching a class or independent of it, librarians will often prepare written materials on the use of specific tools, bibliographies of relevant indexes and reference books, lists of suggested subject headings or descriptors, worksheets to use as the basis of research journals, and exercises to be used either with selected reprints or directly in the library.

The extent of available library instruction services depends on the structure, program, and personnel of a given library. Most librarians are service oriented and want to be responsive to the academic needs of students and faculty. Even where a service is not offered routinely, the staff may be able to provide it in response to a specific request.

There is a national clearinghouse for information related to library instruction programs from which librarians and teaching faculty can borrow sample publications, workbooks, exercises, and other materials. For more information contact: Project LOEX, Center of Educational Resources, Eastern Michigan University, Ypsilanti, MI 48197.

ACCESS TO NEEDED RESOURCES

In recent decades, several factors have fundamentally changed the nature of access to library materials. The increasing amount of available material and the escalating costs of acquiring, processing, and storing it have led to a recognition that the scholarly community today must share resources, and that even the largest libraries can no longer function independently. At the same time, the computer has made it much easier to link information records and thus to know which libraries have the needed items.

Interlibrary loan is the traditional way to obtain material from other libraries. Loan policies are now much less restrictive than formerly, and computerized networks speed the transmission of information. But, since in most cases the materials themselves still need to be transported by mail, interlibrary loan can be slow. Plan ahead.

Borrowing periods for interlibrary loan vary, but are generally about one month. Additional time can occasionally be negotiated, but interlibrary loan librarians are dependent upon one another and are usually anxious not to abuse borrowing limits. Some libraries now levy charges when they provide materials; policies about passing along those charges to the patron vary.

Local networks and consortia have been formed in many regions. Whether formal or informal, these arrangements generally allow patrons to borrow directly from the other members. Knowledge of the contents of the other collections may be gained through an on-line hook-up, a microfiche or printed catalog. In some schools such information is highlighted and used frequently; elsewhere the patron may need to inquire about the availability of such union lists.

The Center for Research Libraries, in Chicago, is a membership organization that warehouses seldom-used research materials and makes them available to members on interlibrary loan. A printed catalog of newspapers is available, and there is a fiche catalog of the entire collection.

OCLC (Ohio Computerized Library Center) is an international organization of college, university, public, and special libraries. Started in the late 1960s, OCLC's major product is an electronic data base that now contains more than eleven million records of books and serials owned by over four thousand American and Canadian libraries. An OCLC terminal provides instant access to the catalogs of these libraries. The data base provides complete bibliographic information and tells which participating libraries own the book. Some libraries provide public access to the OCLC data base; in others, one needs to ask the librarian.

RLIN (Research Libraries Information Network), WLN (Washington Library Network), and other bibliographic utilities have purposes similar to those of OCLC, with variations in membership policies.

LIBRARY EQUIPMENT

Many of the sources discussed in this book are available only in microformat. Acceptance of microform materials and comfort in their use vary widely. Part of that variation is explained by the kind of equipment available and where it is located, part is explained by the degree of support the library gives to its microform facilities and collections, and part may be explained by the age of potential users. The current generation of students, accustomed to equipment, screens, knobs, dials, and reels, does not come to microfilm machines with the anti-machine attitude of an older generation. (They are also less likely to be wearing bifocals, which can increase fatigue among wearers using most microfilm machines.) Some students have come to prefer microforms because they can rely on finding them; they are less likely than print materials to be lost, stolen, mutilated, or misshelved.

Although microform originally meant rolls of microfilm, publishers today seem to be increasingly turning to microfiche. Many people prefer fiche to film because it is simpler to locate (and relocate) specific pages. Because discrete items are usually on separate fiches, it is easier for an entire class to share a file or set. In addition, portable microfiche readers of reasonable quality are available, and some libraries have purchased them for patrons to use at home.

The ability to make photocopies from filmed material in the same fashion as one does from printed material increases the degree of acceptance. Microform reader/printers are available today that produce high-quality, black-on-white photocopies on bond paper.

High-quality microform machines are expensive and, where heavily used, need frequent maintenance and repair—particularly reader/printers. There will certainly be a greater acceptance of microformats in libraries that have enough machines, maintain them well, and locate them near the service hub of the library rather than in a subbasement. Acquiring the proper equipment and keeping it adequately serviced may be somewhat like the question of the chicken and the egg. The administration is unlikely to invest in the equipment if there is no need; patrons are unlikely to use microforms if the available equipment is unsatisfactory. Some degree of faculty pressure applied to library and school administrations might be helpful in these situations.[1]

HINTS FOR A GOOD WORKING RELATIONSHIP WITH THE LIBRARY

Don't:

- Assume that students will know how to find the information they need.
- Request that students use specific items without first checking their availability.

- Send the entire class to look for a single item. After the first person uses it, it will never be on the shelf. If it really is necessary for everyone to use the same volume, discuss it with the librarians first; they may be able to suggest a solution.

- Use published books of library exercises without first checking their applicability in your own library. Most of these books, although well meaning, were designed for the home library of the author and are not completely transferable to another situation. They can be extremely frustrating for students and library staff. (If you would like a library workbook speak to the instruction librarian.)

- Send students on a scavenger hunt. It may sound like fun, but it is generally irrelevant to students' needs and invariably becomes more of a challenge for the reference staff than for the student. (If you would like a library exercise, talk to the instruction librarian about designing one appropriate to the class.)

- Send students to the library with incorrect citations.

- Ask students to use materials so current that they may not be available yet.

- Request an entire class to do research using books on the same subject. Unless your library is exceedingly large or your subject is very broad, most of the students will face only frustration when they encounter shelves already emptied by the first few students. If many people are to research the same narrow subject, it is preferable to limit research to journal articles or reference books that do not circulate.

Do, please:

- Involve the library staff in planning research assignments.

- Check to see that the needed materials are available before recommending them to students.

- Provide the library with a written copy of the assignment and the objectives. Be sure that the objectives and the level of research required are clear to students and librarians.

- Be sure the library gets a copy of suggested topics for research given to students.

- Arrange with the instruction librarian for a course-related lecture for your class.

- When you prepare a reading list, unless your objective is to have each student look up each item in the library catalog, include the classification numbers.[2]

NOTES

1. Eichhorn, "Standards for Public Service of Microform Collections," provides a good discussion of this subject.

2. Every librarian has a variation of this list; one that is similar to mine is: Fink, "What You Ask For Is What You Get: Some Dos and Don'ts for Assigning Research Projects."

4

Teaching Scholarly Documentation

Proper documentation of sources is vital to scholarly communication; the importance of this concept is deeply ingrained in academics. Students, however, tend to regard questions of volume and issue number, precise attribution, quotation marks, and Latin words as merely burdensome detail. This is perhaps understandable; the concern with format and consistency that marks most style manuals emphasizes the mechanical rather than the intellectual problems of documentation. This brief chapter contains suggestions for exercises that show how documentation is used by the scholar and demonstrate the need for precision in the intellectual as well as the mechanical aspects of the process. Some of these exercises can be expanded into more substantial research and writing projects.

THE "WHY" OF DOCUMENTATION

Have students locate one or more scholarly articles cited in footnotes in their textbook. Including a citation that is difficult to trace because it is inaccurate, incomplete, or confusing will make a strong point. Depending on the objectives of the assignment, students can be asked to summarize the article and evaluate the manner in which it was used by the citing author. Questions that might be addressed include: Was the statement used in context? Did the information in the article substantiate what the citing author said? Might other points in the article have been used to advantage? Why did the author choose to cite this article? How has reading the cited material enhanced your understanding?

For a more ambitious project, take a recent, short, scholarly article in your field. Have students go back to some of the sources on which the article was based. Pose questions such as: Would you have used those sources in the same way? Were any ideas or facts taken out of context? Did the author leave undocumented statements that should have been documented? Does the documentation support the author's statements?

THE "HOW" AND "WHEN" OF DOCUMENTATION

A nonstandard item can be used effectively to demonstrate the necessary elements of a citation. After the basics of documentation have been discussed, and one of these exercises undertaken, the instructor might bring to class an item from the college archive (or from a personal collection of ephemera) and ask the class to construct appropriate footnote and bibliography statements. Having had the experience of locating specific items based on footnotes, the class should have a concept of the bibliographic elements needed for adequate identification and an understanding of the need for precise description of those elements.

As an exercise in when to document statements, students can be asked to take a newspaper or popular magazine article (perhaps from several years ago) and indicate where documentation of the statements would be necessary if this were a scholarly article. This comparatively simple exercise can teach important lessons.

NOTE

1. Two variations of this type of exercise are described by Cassara, "The Student as Detective: An Undergraduate Exercise in Historiographical Research," and by Faber, "Alternatives to the Term Paper."

PART II

5

Presenting the Research:
Alternatives to the Term Paper Format

Although librarians' primary concern in the research/writing process is with the research, we are necessarily aware of the formats in which that research is presented. Over the years many innovative approaches have been devised by teachers of writing and others for the presentation of research findings.[1]

This chapter discusses formats for student writing that provide alternatives to the traditional term paper. They can be used with the usual undergraduate sources of information—books and journal articles—or with some of the less often used sources discussed in the following section of this book. Most of these ideas come from others; a few are my own. Nothing here is in any way revolutionary as a writing form; the attempt is rather to summarize some of the possibilities. Although the specific advantages of these formats vary, they share the advantage that the student writer is unlikely to hand in unoriginal work.

PERSONAL WRITINGS: LETTERS, DIARIES, JOURNALS

These forms of personal writings are generally used to communicate feelings, observations, or information, either for oneself or for another.

In recent years the Writing Across the Curriculum movement has promoted the keeping of diaries and journals to increase the amount of students' writing. Used to stimulate ease in writing, and frequently assigned with the understanding that they will not be graded, such journals may record reactions to class discussion or to assigned readings, or be limited to the student's personal ideas and speculations. Since such journals record only the writer's thoughts and actions, they are unrelated to any research objectives.

By having the student pretend to be someone else, however, this same journal format can become a framework within which to present researched information. Because of its many possible variations, this approach is applicable to courses in almost all subject areas as well as to basic composition courses. The approach is perhaps most useful when only a small amount of writing is desired. The level of research required to complete the assignment can range from minimal to a depth appropriate for advanced classes.

A few possibilities:

- Diary entries or letters as they might have been written by a person representative of a particular group or a particular viewpoint describing or analyzing an actual place, event, or situation. For example: the diary of a prisoner in 1880 describing life in the prison; a letter from an Irish immigrant giving his view of Boston in 1850, or from a Vietnamese immigrant talking about New York City in 1980; a letter from a factory worker describing the factory and working conditions in 1850, 1890, 1932, or 1942; diary entries of an academic painter on seeing an Impressionist painting in 1880.

- A diary or letter as it might have been written by an actual historical person about a real event or situation. Such an assignment can call for straight description or for analysis and commentary; the event can be described in a letter and analyzed in a journal entry. The student researcher must gather enough information about the event to be able to describe or analyze it and must have enough biographical information about the "author" to make the description plausible.

- In another variation of this format, students compose diary entries or letters as they might have been written by a fictional character. In order to do this, the student needs, in addition to information about the event, sufficient insight into the fictional character to make the description plausible.

As a format for written assignments, the diary, journal, and letter have the advantage of flexibility and variable length; the assignment can call for a one-page journal entry, an exchange of two letters or ten, or diary entries covering one day, one year, or several decades. Content can vary from a simple description of a single event to an analysis of a lengthy or complex social or political controversy.

Because the essence of these formats is the immediacy of the observation to the event described, reading contemporary newspaper and magazine reportage would be helpful. For that reason, these formats may be particularly useful when research objectives include, or are even limited to, the use of such sources and their indexes. The research objectives can be deepened by requesting students to locate an actual diary or letters written by persons who described or participated in the event. (See Chapter 10 for sources for locating diaries, Chapter 7 for newspapers and periodicals.)

NEWSPAPERS: ARTICLES, EDITORIALS, NEWS CONFERENCES

Like personal communications, these formats have the advantage of varying greatly in length. The amount and type of research they require can also vary. The following alternatives are applicable in a historical context or a contemporary one.

The "Objective" Newspaper Story

Students can be asked to write a newspaper article describing an event—political, social, cultural, whatever suits the objectives—based on their research. The assignment can be limited to one or two articles, or it can be more extensive. This is a good exercise in critical reading and in summarizing. The assignment gains added interest if several people research the same event in different sources and compare the "objective" newspaper stories that result.

Newspaper Articles as "Rewrites"

Having completed a traditional term paper, students can be asked to rewrite it into a short newspaper article. Alternatively, they can be asked to rewrite another student's research report as a newspaper article.

Editorial or Column of Opinion

Research requirements for writing editorials are the same as for a straight newspaper story, although the amount of reading required may be greater. Editorial writing requires analysis of facts rather than just summarizing them. Writing editorials in a historical context might be particularly stimulating; for example, an editorial in opposition to the Declaration of Independence, women's suffrage, or the Social Security laws.

Letters to the editor are another variation on this theme. Editorial writers can be asked to respond to letters to the editor, either those written by classmates, or those that actually appeared in newspapers.

Producing an Entire Newspaper

A stimulating project for a group or class would be to produce an entire newspaper. Here again, the framework can be either the real or a fictional world.

For example:

- Suppose the group of people gathered at Jane Austen's Mansfield Park had decided on a literary rather than a theatrical production. They could have produced a "journal" containing news of the day: political news, both national and international; a gossip column about characters in the novel and contemporary figures; an obituary column giving biographical material about Jane Austen or others; and perhaps a letter from Sir Thomas Bertram describing his travels in Antigua.

- A group of Pennsylvania Quakers might produce an abolitionist newspaper containing descriptions of actual slave revolts, biographical notes about abolitionist leaders, editorials giving reasons for opposition to slavery, letters to the editor written by free Negroes, excerpts from travel diaries, and illustrations. The items to be included can be taken from periodicals of the period, written by students based on reading similar articles, or a combination of both.

The following are additional variations suitable for newspaper projects:

- The event reported on could be an actual event or a fictionalized pastiche of similar events.

- For newspapers reflecting a designated historical period, students could write their articles about the event using only information available at the time (drawing on newspapers, magazines, and perhaps diaries and journals) or they could use textbooks and other secondary sources and make the article a reconstruction based on today's information. An alternative would have the class produce two newspapers, one based on primary sources, one on secondary sources.

News Conferences

These offer good opportunities to add depth to research and thus might work particularly well with advanced students. A "verbatim" transcript or an analytical description of a news conference can serve as a format for simulated interviews with well-known people of any period. What questions would contemporaries have asked? What questions would we now, with hindsight, want to ask? How would contemporary answers have differed from those that might be given today? Here students have an opportunity to take a rigorous, analytical approach, both in terms of the questions to be asked and the information contained in the answers.

COMPILATIONS: ANTHOLOGIES, SOURCEBOOKS, SCRAPBOOKS

The following projects also allow for variation in the amount of research and writing required, although they tend to require more research in relation to writing than other formats. They can prove particularly useful as spurs to evaluative and critical thinking.

Anthologies

The model for this format is the annotated book of readings with which most students are familiar. In this case, however, rather than being given the anthology, they are asked to compile it themselves. The assignment can limit the acceptable content of the anthology to scholarly articles written within the last ten years, or it can be broadened to include chapters or excerpts from monographs and significant older materials.

Students should be asked to write an introduction to the anthology that would display an overall understanding of the subject. In addition, each item should be described, and an explanation given as to why it is included. The assignment could also require a bibliography of items considered for inclusion as well as copies of the items selected.

In any subject course in which students would benefit from finding and reading a variety of scholarly articles, such an assignment would guarantee that they use their library skills to locate the articles, their critical reading skills to make the selections, and a variety of writing skills to produce the introduction, the summaries, and the explanations.

Sourcebooks

The concept of the student-produced anthology can be expanded into a student-produced sourcebook containing some combination of contemporaneous newspaper or magazine articles, documents, excerpts from diaries and speeches, reports, illustrations, and selections from secondary sources. Research objectives set for the assignment would determine the content of the sourcebook.

Scrapbooks

An anthology or sourcebook needs to have order, selection, and scholarly perspective imposed on its contents; a scrapbook, by contrast, is usually the work of an interested person who assembles relevant materials with no thought for the scholarly apparatus of introduction and written evaluation. However, for the purposes of classroom assignments students could be asked to compile the sort of scrapbook that would have been done by another person—either fictional or real—and provide a written justification for the items selected. For example: the scrapbook Jacob Riis might have compiled to illustrate the need for child-labor laws would probably contain pictures and newspaper and magazine articles. It might also have excerpts from diaries and letters, and from government documents. The scrapbook kept by Nick Carraway, the narrator in F. Scott Fitzgerald's *The Great Gatsby*, might include excerpts from congressional debates about Prohibition, as well as articles describing the bootlegging and speakeasies that resulted.

Pictorial Anthologies

The model for this is any good pictorial history. It can be a visual equivalent of the anthology or scrapbook format discussed previously, with pictures drawn from a variety of sources. Research would involve locating the illustrations and gathering enough information to write informative captions and an introductory essay. (See Chapter 11.)

Group Projects

Anthologies, sourcebooks, and scrapbooks can make stimulating group projects. Each student or group of students works on a different problem; the resulting anthologies can then be exchanged, thereby increasing the amount of material each person reads without increasing research time. Reading their classmates' anthologies might be more stimulating than reading similar material in a textbook or reader. At the end of the semester students can write brief book reviews of several of the anthologies.

LEAFLETS AND PAMPHLETS

Leaflets and pamphlets, formats that could generate a great deal of student enthusiasm, can be used to meet a variety of research objectives. They require critical judgment and clear, concise writing.

Production of a leaflet (or a short pamphlet) taking sides on a given issue obviously requires knowledge of the questions involved; even a short leaflet can be written only by a person who has gathered the facts. Once the facts are gathered, selecting the most persuasive arguments and presenting them in one page is in itself a valuable experience. The leaflet can be combined with a longer writing assignment designed around a controversial issue.

In subject classes, controversial issues can be chosen to support curriculum objectives. Leaflets and short pamphlets can be individual projects designed to increase each student's understanding of a particular issue, or group efforts intended to stimulate class discussion and interaction. Groups of students can be asked to produce leaflets on each side of the issue and debate them, or one side can produce its leaflets first, after which the opposition can write a response.

Appropriate controversies for composition classes can range from specific events (The Bay of Pigs invasion, the Teapot Dome scandal) to broad, presumably settled, issues (slavery, women's suffrage, compulsory education), historical topics still of concern (the death penalty, immigration, prayer in public schools) or the newer controversies (compulsory drug testing, reverse discrimination). For historical controversies that still plague us, it might be interesting to have some students produce leaflets as they would have been written in the 19th century, and others as they would appear today.

Research requirements for this type of assignment can vary greatly. Leaflets can be written on the basis of reading monographs and scholarly articles, or newspapers and popular magazine articles. For historical controversies the information can be ex post facto or limited to what was available at the time. In any case, research objectives can be extended and arguments strengthened if the assignment calls for the inclusion of statistics. Some projects will become even more interesting if a contemporary illustration is requested.

One further variation that students might find stimulating requires dividing the class into several groups: each group is assigned to gather information about a different issue and then give the information to another group to do the writing. The writers are free to request their researchers to supply missing information. The researchers are free to question the writers' conclusions if they feel information supplied does not warrant the conclusions drawn. This type of role changing and interaction will stimulate a more critical attitude toward information gathering and presentation.

NOTE

1. Some of the ideas in this chapter are adapted from: Faber, "Alternatives to the Term Paper," and Huber and Lewis, "Tired of Term Papers? Options for Librarians and Professors."

PART III

6

The Undergraduate Researcher
and Primary Sources

Until recently, the most exciting aspect of library research—the glean-
ing and processing of information from primary sources—was an activity limited to "serious" scholars because of the rarity and location of
the documents. Today, microforms and reprint publishers have made
research in primary sources possible for all, including undergraduates.
This chapter tells how to identify and locate appropriate primary
sources and suggests guidelines for their use by undergraduates. Specific titles are discussed in later chapters.[1] Although most of the
sources discussed in this chapter and following chapters fall into the
category of historical resources, projects and approaches will be suggested that are appropriate for use in other humanities and social science disciplines.

WHAT IS A PRIMARY SOURCE?

To understand what research really is, students need to understand
the difference between primary sources—the raw data of scholarship—
and secondary sources—the works of analysis and synthesis with which
they are most familiar. They need to know that primary sources vary
greatly in type and format and are different for different disciplines.
For the historian, a primary source can be a handwritten letter, a
printed book or newspaper, or a stone tablet; for the political scientist,
it can be a computer printout of voting records or an annual report of

a government agency; for a sociologist, a returned survey form or a map of the city; for a literary scholar, a work of fiction, the original manuscript of that work, or the first printed reviews of it.

Part of the confusion that arises when students discuss primary sources results from a failure to recognize that some documents can be either a primary source or a secondary source depending on when and how they are used. The *Encyclopedia of Social Reform*, published in 1897, was a secondary source when written; today it is a primary source for the student interested in the history of social science. Today's editorial suggesting solutions to problems of prison overcrowding may be a secondary source for suggested solutions and a primary source for contemporary attitudes; in fifty years it could be a primary source for either.

Primary sources today take many forms. They may be in their original form (the handwritten letter, the original paper copy of the magazine, the ledger book of the business), in microform (an exact photocopy of the original on film), or bound (either a photoreproduction of the original or a transcription of the words—the intellectual content—onto modern paper).

WHY INTRODUCE PRIMARY SOURCES TO UNDERGRADUATES?

There are three good reasons to refer undergraduates to primary sources: first, students enjoy them; second, they are basic to scholarship; and third, they can be used effectively to stimulate a critical approach to reading and thinking.

Evidence from librarians and from classroom teachers makes clear that students enjoy the challenge of going directly to the sources used by scholars and attempting to reconstruct the life, attitudes, and events of an earlier period. For those who have previously experienced boredom or failure with research projects, using primary sources can put research into a new and welcome perspective.

Primary sources underlie scholarship. Works of analysis and synthesis are obviously significant to both scholar and student, but students— whether looking toward further academic work or not—should understand the significance of the documentary material on which those secondary works are based. They should discover for themselves that primary sources and primary research are what scholarship is about, and that this kind of digging, in addition to being the "nitty-gritty," is also fun.

Many primary sources have purposes that are familiar to students. Students understand the role of letters, diaries, and newspapers, although they will likely be less familiar with annual reports and the working papers of an organization. When using these sources from another era, however, although the purpose may be familiar, the language and the format will be unfamiliar. Paradoxically, this unfamiliarity can make it easier to break away from familiar reading patterns. The physical unfamiliarity may lead students to take a more analytical approach to reading than the approach they take to their accustomed reading material.

The closer we can bring students to sources in their original form, the more profitable the experience is likely to be. Reprints, although retaining the intellectual content, may lose some of the immediacy— the quaking hand, the ink blot, frequently the illustrations—of the original. Thus, microforms or photoreproductions are probably better than a reprint reset in modern type. On the other hand, some documents are so difficult to read in the original that after students have extracted the original "flavor," they may be better off working from transcriptions.

In addition, research in primary sources, where the way in which material is read can be more important than the amount read, emphasizes that thinking, rather than reading, is the essence of research.

Undergraduates will naturally use primary materials differently from the way experienced scholars use them. We don't expect original research—in the sense of new discoveries—from undergraduates. But they are fully capable of "discovering" a fact within a document; of drawing inferences from statements left unsaid; of integrating information derived from a variety of resources, and of savoring the excitement and intellectual stimulation that comes from doing so. For the undergraduate making the discovery all this is new; what matter if scholars in the field have known about it for years?

Among the most commonly available primary sources are: newspapers and magazines (discussed in Chapter 7); archives, annual reports, and statistical sources (discussed in Chapter 8); legal sources (discussed in Chapter 9); and autobiographical sources (discussed, along with biographical sources, in Chapter 10).

IDENTIFYING AVAILABLE PRIMARY SOURCES

Primary Sources in Microform

The largest number of sources is available on microform. Almost everything available in this format is listed in:

Guide to Microforms in Print, Incorporating International Microforms in Print: Subject Guide to Microforms in Print. Westport, CT: Meckler Publishing, 1978- . Annual.

This guide is a cumulative listing of books, journals, newspapers, archival materials, and collections currently available in microformat. Thousands of titles are included. The subject guide is arranged by title within broad categories such as: music; architecture; U.S. history, war with Spain to the present; and American literature. There is a more detailed index to the coverage within the broad categories, but reference is to the category and not to the individual item. Because of this arrangement careful reading of a significant number of entries is sometimes necessary in order to locate those of potential interest. Entries in both the basic volume and the subject guide include the publisher's name and sometimes the price, but they are not annotated in any way.

Less complete but generally more useful is:

Dodge, Suzanne Cates. *Microform Research Collections: A Guide.* 2d edition. Westport, CT: Meckler Publishing, 1984.

This valuable book is a recommended first step in any attempt to find appropriate materials in microformat. It analyzes more than 350 of what the editor has determined to be the most significant of the large microform sets. Included for each set is a full description of the content and arrangement, a listing of available indexes and finding aids, citations to reviews, physical descriptions, and prices. In addition, there are author, title, and detailed subject indexes.

A basic reviewing medium for microform publications is:

Microform Review. Westport, CT: Meckler Publishing, 1972- . Quarterly.

Its reviews are substantial in length and very informative. In addition to its own yearly indexes, it is indexed in *Library Literature* and *Current Index to Journals in Education (CIJE).*

Publishers' catalogs. Although obviously intended to sell the microform sets, the descriptions in these catalogs are frequently the best guide to what is in the set. There are many small micropublishers, but a few large ones presently dominate the field. The acquisitions depart-

ment of your library may have a set of these catalogs, or you can request them directly.

Among the major microform publishers are:

- Chadwyck-Healey Inc., 1021 Prince St., Alexandria, VA 22314. 703-683-5890.
  (They are particularly strong in pictorial sources.)
- Clearwater Publishing, 1995 Broadway, New York, NY 10023.
- National Archives, Pennsylvania Ave. & 8th St. NW, Washington, DC 20408.
  202-523-3218.
- Research Publications, 12 Lunar Drive/Drawer AB, Woodbridge, CT 06525.
  203-297-3893; 800-REACH-RP.
- University Microfilms International, 3000 N. Zeeb Rd., Ann Arbor, MI 48106.
  313-761-4700; 800-423-6108.
- University Publications of America, 44 North Market St., Frederick, MD 21701.
  301-694-0100; 800-692-6300.

Primary Sources in Print

These may be photoreproductions of entire books, or collections of
documents. The simplest way to find out what is available is to check
the subject listings in *Books in Print* and in the library catalog, looking
for the subdivision *Sources*.

When using the library catalog (or *Books in Print*) remember that
catalogers always use the most specific subject heading possible to
identify an item; for example: U.S. FOREIGN RELATIONS—REVO-
LUTION, 1775-1783—SOURCES, or EDUCATION—GREAT BRI-
TAIN—HISTORY—SOURCES.

Use of the SOURCES subdivision will not help to locate monographs. However, many of the most interesting of these are now available in reprint series, and may be identified through *Books in Series*,
Fourth ed., 4 vols., New York: R. R. Bowker Company, 1985.

Among the most active reprint publishers are:

- AMS Press, 56 East 13 St., New York, NY 10003
- Arno Press, 3 Park Ave., New York, NY 10017
- Burt Franklin, 235 East 44 St., New York, NY 10017
- Da Capo Press, 227 West 17 St., New York, NY 10011
- Garland Publishing, Inc., 136 Madison Ave., New York, NY 10016
- Kraus Reprint & Periodicals (KRP), Rt. 100, Millwood, NY 10546

Published collections of primary sources are convenient, but this very convenience changes the nature of the research experience. Not only have the documents been preselected, but the notes and introductory essays that generally accompany these collections are such that students may be "spared" the need to do precisely the kind of background research that would develop their library research skills. At times, however, published collections can be useful supplements to unedited sources.

Primary Sources in Their Original Form

Don't overlook the obvious. Every community has some primary sources buried somewhere. Check with the archivist or special collections librarian in your own and other local colleges. Check the local historical society, even if it is a small one. Check the local public library and the city archives. Student researchers in smaller towns and cities may gain access to archival materials more easily than those in our larger cities.

OBTAINING THE NEEDED MATERIAL

Since cataloging policies for microforms and special collections vary greatly, the best advice about ascertaining availability is: don't make assumptions about your own library; always check with the staff. In a large library it may be wise to check with librarians in charge of collection development, serials, microforms, and special collections, as well as the subject specialists in the reference department.

Materials not in the home library may still be available for your students. Today many libraries are members of local or regional consortia that combine resources to purchase expensive or low-demand research materials. These jointly owned materials may be entered in the individual library's catalog or listed separately. In other instances, although materials may not be jointly owned, neighboring institutions will agree to welcome your students. In these days of on-line and microfiche libraries, it is often possible to check in your own library for catalogs and other holding lists of neighboring schools.

If you cannot find what you want locally, you may be able to obtain it on interlibrary loan. Although not every library will lend microfilm, many now do so. If normal interlibrary loan is not feasible, the Center for Research Libraries is another option. (See the discussion in Chapter 3.)

STRATEGIES FOR INTRODUCING PRIMARY SOURCES

Some general questions may help students in their initial approach to an unfamiliar primary source; other questions will arise naturally from the specific source.

- When was the document written? If there is no date, what elements within it can help to establish a date?

- Who wrote it? If there is no obvious author, are there hints in the document that indicate the author's class, occupation, sex, or age?

- What was the purpose of the document? (Official communication, unofficial communication, record keeping, propaganda, publicity, and so on.)

- For whom was it written? Is there an implied or "hidden" audience as well as an openly intended audience?

- Are there implicit assumptions? Did the original readers know or assume things not stated in the document?

- Some implicit assumptions are clear. Might there be others? What hints point to this?

- Is the source reliable? The usual criteria for evaluating the reliability (or authority) of primary sources are (1) the closer the source is to the activity documented, the better it is as a record of the activity, and (2) the less selectivity involved in documenting the event, the more reliable is that documentation.

Some of the suggestions below might be useful in structuring the assignments. Which will be appropriate will vary with the sources, the assignments, and the level of the class.

- Read through the document quickly; write one paragraph of initial impressions.

- Read the document carefully and outline it; summarize it; analyze it; paraphrase it.

- In official documents, what is left out is frequently as important as what is included. Ask students to list categories or specific items of information that may have been omitted.

- If the document is a newspaper report, analyze it in terms of selectivity of reporting: Is there a point of view? What was omitted? What could have been done to make this a more objective view?

- Make a list of all unfamiliar words. Are familiar words used in an unfamiliar fashion? Check them in *Oxford English Dictionary*, and appropriate slang dictionaries (see list at end of this chapter).

- Make a list of all unfamiliar names and places. Check them in the appropriate sources (see list at end of this chapter).

- Read the document carefully and list: statements that you know are true, statements you think are probably true, statements that are probably untrue, and statements that are opinions.

- In what ways does this document differ from a similar one today? Rewrite it (or a part of it) in an appropriate style for today.

- Compare the document with a similar one from another period or another place.

- Where possible, locate additional contemporary information about the person, incident, or institution (for example, for a prison annual report, locate information about that prison in newspapers and periodicals of the time; for a newspaper report of an event, locate a magazine story about it or a contemporary biographical portrait of the people involved; for an archive, locate newspaper and magazine stories about the institution).

- Research the incident or institution in secondary sources. This can be a large-scale hunt or a very limited one.

- Write an analysis of the document as contemporary readers might have seen it; write an analysis of the document based on what we know today.

- Rewrite the article or document in a more "objective" fashion. Additional information can be supplied from the imagination or located through research.

- For students with no experience in this type of analytical reading, or for developmental classes, an initial in-class exercise in "reading between the lines" might be helpful. It could be based on a single photocopied sample distributed in class.

PUTTING THE PRIMARY SOURCES IN PERSPECTIVE: SECONDARY REFERENCE SOURCES TO HELP STUDENTS USE PRIMARY SOURCES

Scholars approach primary sources with an understanding of the era and circumstances that produced them. Undergraduates who lack that frame of reference must be taught about resources that can provide sufficient background information to enable them to understand the primary sources.

The need to place the document in context and to understand individual elements within it is in fact a major value of this kind of research. Appropriately structured, these assignments provide an unparalleled opportunity for students to become acquainted with a broad range of standard reference sources that they will use for many future projects. And they will gain this knowledge within the context of a purpose—a "need to know"—rather than as a meaningless and frustrating scavenger hunt.

The following list of sources may be useful to provide overviews and to answer factual questions that arise while using the primary sources discussed in this book. The list is merely suggestive; it is arranged by generic type of source, with a few specific titles under each type. Other titles may be better for specific projects. For suggestions consult the reference librarians in your library.

ENCYCLOPEDIAS

Students frequently need to be reassured that there is an appropriate use for encyclopedias; a knowledge of available subject encyclopedias and when to use them is one of the most useful research skills they can develop. They need to be taught that an encyclopedia article can provide the necessary overview or framework within which to place specific documents or ideas. Such articles may also provide an historical introduction, identify important names and movements, and give a sense of the significant controversies of the period or subject in question.

There are dozens of useful subject encyclopedias; the following ones have been selected to demonstrate the range of what is available.

Dictionary of Literary Biography. 45 vols. Detroit: Gale Research Co., 1978- .

Encyclopedia of American Journalism. New York: Facts on File, 1983.

Encyclopedia of American Political History. 3 vols. New York: Scribners, 1984.

Encyclopedia of American Religions. 2 vols. Wilmington, NC: McGrath Pub., 1978.

Encyclopedia of Bioethics. 4 vols. New York: Free Press, 1978.

Encyclopedia of Crime and Justice. 4 vols. New York: Free Press, 1983.

Encyclopedia of Education. New York: Macmillan, 1971.

Encyclopedia of World Art. 15 vols. New York: McGraw-Hill, 1968.

Greenwood Encyclopedia of American Institutions: Labor Unions. Westport, CT: Greenwood Press, 1977.

Harvard Encyclopedia of American Ethnic Groups. Cambridge, MA: Belknap Press, 1980.

The Twentieth Century. 20 vols. Milwaukee, WI: Purnell Reference Books, 1979.

Useful encyclopedias related to law have been listed in the chapter on legal resources.

BIOGRAPHICAL DIRECTORIES

The two widely available comprehensive American biographical directories are:

Dictionary of American Biography. 20 vols. plus index. New York:
    Scribner, 1928-1937. Reprint ed.: 10 vols. plus 7 vols. supple-
    ments. New York: Scribner, 1943.

National Cyclopedia of American Biography. 63 vols. Ann Arbor, MI:
    University Microfilms, 1892-1984.

The basic volumes of this set were issued in 1892. The flavor of the
set is clear from the original subtitle: ... *being the History of the
United States, as illustrated in the lives of the founders, builders, and
defenders of the Republic, and of the men and women who are doing
the work and moulding the thought of the present time. Edited by
Distinguished biographers, selected from each state, revised and ap-
proved by the most eminent historians, scholars and statesmen of the
day.*

This is a particularly useful set for students researching some of the
lesser-known people of the nineteenth century. The articles were written from information supplied by the biographees or their families.
The set is not arranged alphabetically so must be used through the
indexes.

Notable American Women, 1607-1950: A Biographical Dictionary.
    Cambridge, MA: Harvard University Press, 1971.
*Notable American Women, The Modern Period: A Biographical Dic-
    tionary.* Cambridge, MA: Harvard University Press, 1980.
    These are frequently needed supplements to the older sets.

There are, in addition to the few sets discussed here, the full range
of *Who's Who* volumes, plus hundreds of special-interest biographical
directories, running from the *Dictionary of American Temperance
Biography,* Westport, CT: Greenwood Press, 1984, to the *Biographical Dictionary of American Cult and Sect Leaders,* New York: Garland
Publishing, 1986, to the *Biographical Dictionary of the Confederacy,*
Westport, CT: Greenwood Press, 1977.

A set of finding aids for biographical information that can be particularly helpful when researching relatively unknown individuals is:

*Biography and Genealogy Master Index: A Consolidated Index to
    more than 3,200,000 Biographical Sketches in over 350 Current
    and Retrospective Biographical Dictionaries.* 2d ed. Detroit: Gale
    Research Co., 1984.
*Biography and Genealogy Master Index, 1981-1985 Cumulation: A
    Consolidated Index to more than 2,250,000 Biographical
    Sketches in 215 Current and Retrospective Biographical Dic-
    tionaries.* Detroit: Gale Research Co., 1985.

This mammoth set together indexes almost five and a half million biographical sketches. A good place to start when looking for information about obscure people, it is available on-line through *Dialog* as well as in hard copy. The entries do not give the biographical information, but provide citations to the directories indexed. Many libraries may find it more cost-effective to access this on-line as needed rather than purchase the published set.

Historical Biographical Dictionaries Master Index: A Consolidated Index to Biographical Information Concerning Historical Personages in over 35 of the Principal Retrospective Biographical Dictionaries. Detroit: Gale Research Co., 1980.

This smaller set is drawn from the larger one; it is obviously less costly, and, though containing much less data than the master index may be adequate for 19th-century American biographees.

Personal Name Index to the New York Times Index.

This is a cumulative index to all names, whether used as entries or not, that appear in the *New York Times Index*. See discussion in Chapter 7.

HISTORICAL DICTIONARIES

The following might provide information to supplement that in the subject encyclopedias:

Grun, Bernard. *The Timetables of History: A Horizontal Linkage of People and Events.* New York: Simon and Schuster, 1975.

A graphic, year-by-year presentation of highlights of political, social, cultural, intellectual, scientific, and technological developments.

Morris, Richard B., ed. *Encyclopedia of American History.* 6th ed. New York: Harper & Row, 1982.

STATISTICS

The key secondary sources for statistics about the United States are:

Historical Statistics of the United States, Colonial Times to 1970. 2 vols. Washington, DC: Government Printing Office, 1976.

Statistical Abstract of the United States. Washington, DC: Government Printing Office, 1878- . Annual.

Mitchell, B.R. *European Historical Statistics, 1750-1975.* New York: Facts on File, 1980.

World Almanac, 1868-1893. Cleveland, OH: Bell and Howell Micro-
photo Division, 1973. Microfiche.

Almanacs are always useful for facts and figures. Both secondary
source and primary source, this set can provide students with many
insights into the nineteenth century.

DICTIONARIES

Oxford English Dictionary. 13 vols. Oxford: Clarendon Press, 1933.

Beloved by English scholars, this dictionary will prove useful to
students tracing changes in the meaning of words.

Partridge, Eric. *The Macmillan Dictionary of Historical Slang.* Abridged
by Jacqueline Simpson. New York: Macmillan, 1974.

Farmer, J. S., and W. E. Henley. *Slang and Its Analogues.* With an Introduction by Theodore M. Bernstein. New York: Arno, 1970.
The original edition of this work was published from 1890 to 1904.

NOTE

1. Assignments using primary sources are discussed in: Cassara, "The Student
as Detective: An Undergraduate Exercise in Historiographical Research," Estus,
Hickey, McClymer, and Moynihan, *Creating Effective Community History Assignments,* McClain and Clegg, "Words, Records, and Beyond: Studying About
Local Ethnic Groups Through Primary Sources," Monkkonen, "Involving Survey Students in Primary Research," Walker, "Teaching the Method of History:
A Documentary Exercise."

7

Primary Sources:
Newspapers and Magazines of the
19th and Early 20th Centuries

Most undergraduates, if they stopped to think about it, would realize that there were newspapers and magazines in the 19th century. Librarians, however, can attest to the surprise of many students when they realize that they can read and use periodicals published fifty or a hundred years ago almost as easily as they can those that were published last year.

These 19th- and early 20th-century newspapers and magazines provide an excellent introduction to primary sources for the undergraduate researcher. Our discussion of primary sources starts with them because:

- students enjoy using them;
- they are widely available;
- their format and purpose are familiar to students;
- the research skills required to use them are readily transferable to projects in more traditional sources;
- they give students the experience of researching primary sources in their original format without involving them in the difficulties of reading handwritten diaries or letters;
- they are adaptable to many different content and skills objectives and are suitable for developmental writing courses as well as upper-level research courses;
- they can be utilized effectively in assignments of almost any length.

Strategies that would be helpful in introducing these materials to students, and suggestions for structuring the assignment, are given in Chapter 6.

WHERE DO THESE SOURCES FIT IN THE CURRICULUM?–SELECTING TOPICS

Subject Classes

Periodicals of the 19th and early 20th centuries can be used to good effect in almost any subject course. Students of literature, music, and drama could research reviews of specific works or read general articles to determine popular attitudes and tastes. The student of art history might be fascinated by American art criticism of the 19th century. For the student of economics, research into child labor, or the ten-hour-day movement, would hold a similar fascination. The student of contemporary politics could delve into any one of dozens of examples of political corruption. Youth gangs of the 1860s is a likely topic for a sociology or criminal justice class. In brief, almost any course in which it is desirable for students to gain some historical perspective could make good use of these sources.

Newspapers and magazines of the 19th and early 20th centuries have also proved to be valuable introductory research sources in literature classes where it is felt that students will neither enjoy nor benefit from large doses of literary analysis and criticism. Novels and stories set in that period, particularly those with plots that rely on the social background or include historical characters or events, are greatly enriched for the student who reads about the events, people, and situations in newspapers and magazines of the period.

English Composition and Developmental Writing Courses

It is perhaps in basic composition and developmental writing classes that these early newspapers and magazines can be most useful; they offer almost unlimited answers to the perennial question of what to write about and are a virtual guarantee that the paper will be the student's own.

Following are several useful approaches to selecting topics for these classes.

–*One of today's controversies as it was viewed in an earlier period:* capital punishment; political corruption; crime; juvenile delinquency; immigrant and ethnic groups; police behavior.

—*Controversies of yesteryear that are no longer considered controversial (or are they?):* evolution, racial and ethnic discrimination; women's rights; right to strike; treatment of criminals, orphans, the insane, the retarded, the elderly.

—*Problems of earlier periods that are no longer problems:* pure milk; tuberculosis (particularly interesting in view of the current concern with AIDS); child labor; imprisonment for debt; slavery.

—*Cultural events:* Armory Show of Modern Art; reviews of famous plays or books; art show reviews; musical performance reviews; famous performers (Booth, Paganini, Caruso).

—*Literature:* Reviews of performances of Ibsen, Shakespeare; biographies of authors; nonfiction background for works of fiction set in the 19th or early 20th century.

—*The broad picture:* The most general topics, such as education, health and hygiene, advertising, and the role of women could be explored.

—*Spectacular and headline events:* Natural and political disasters, riots, strikes, fires, murders, and mysteries are high-interest topics requiring little background information. They will be particularly useful wherever low-reading, high-interest research topics are appropriate. Appendix A lists a selection of headline events of the 19th and 20th centuries which might be considered.

Spectacular topics that seem to work best (1) extend over a long enough period of time so that it is necessary to use indexes to locate at least some of the articles; (2) are complex enough so that students need to sift, evaluate, and organize the material; (3) illuminate some aspect of social, cultural, or technological history; and (4) do not require a great deal of background information.[1]

Instructors interested in topics of this type will find the following book extremely useful:

Kraus, W. Keith. *Murder, Mischief and Mayhem: A Process for Creative Research Papers.* Urbana, IL: National Council of Teachers of English, 1978.

Topics in this book were selected by the author from the *New York Times Index*; they can all be researched through the *Times* and are complex enough to require evaluation and organization of information as well as research in the newspaper over a period of time. There are ninety murders, fifty-seven riots, mysteries, adventures, and other events from which to select. Dates and brief annotations are given for each topic.

Interesting topics of a different type can be suggested by:

Wallechinsky, David, and Irving Wallace. *The People's Almanac.* New York: Doubleday, 1975. *The People's Almanac #2.* New York:

Morrow, 1978. *The People's Almanac #3.* New York: Morrow, 1981.

The stated purpose of this series is to present the people and events left out of the standard almanacs which concentrate on major political events and wealthy and famous people. Although this criterion is not the only one for inclusion in this series, we do find lists such as "Great Works of Art Which Were Greeted by Bad Reviews," "Footnote People in World History," "Sideshow of Popular and Offbeat Performing and Creative Artists," and "Excesses of the Rich" (all from #3).

Lists of natural disasters and famous fires and riots may be found in most standard almanacs.

BASIC APPROACHES TO THE RESEARCH

Two basic research approaches are applicable to this material: (1) the use of standard library finding tools, that is, indexes, and (2) browsing. The use of indexes is highly recommended because it is time-efficient and because it develops a skill transferable to other library research projects. Among the values of research projects utilizing late 19th- and early 20th-century newspapers and magazines is that they can combine research in primary sources with practice in the use of periodical and newspaper indexes.

For undergraduate researchers, the ability to use periodical and newspaper indexes efficiently and effectively is one of the most valuable of library research skills. Regardless of the period or subject being researched, effective use of the indexes requires clear and imaginative thinking, as well as precision and care. For obvious reasons these requirements are particularly important when using indexes compiled during the 19th century.

Although many periodicals of this period are indexed, many more, perhaps equally interesting, are not. For these, the only recourse is to go directly to the publication. Browsing, although not generally suggested as a research strategy for undergraduates, is a legitimate research strategy and is often the only way to find the requisite information.

PERIODICAL INDEXES

Indexes to 19th-Century Popular Magazines

Nineteenth Century Readers' Guide to Periodical Literature. 2 vols. New York: H. W. Wilson, 1944.

Covering a period rich in social progress, 1880 to 1900, this index was actually compiled in 1944 and is identical in format to the familiar *Readers' Guide*. It is probably the best introduction to accessing information from an earlier period because its familiar format makes it easy to use, its terminology is consistent, and it covers the entire twenty-year period in one cumulation. Libraries that do not own this set might consider purchasing it if requested to do so.

Poole's Index to Periodical Literature, 1802-1906. 6 vols. Rev. ed., reprinted. Gloucester, MA: Peter Smith, 1958.

The basic set, in two parts, covers 1802 to 1881. The entire set may be purchased for $252, or individual volumes may be purchased separately.

Mr. Poole, a librarian at Yale University, began compiling his index in 1848. The third edition of the basic volume, covering 1802 to 1881, was published in 1882 and is the foundation for the reprint edition.

Although this set is not difficult to use, the indexing lacks the consistency and uniformity that today's researchers have come to expect. Students using *Poole's* need to know that subject headings as we know them today are a 20th-century invention. Periodical indexes compiled in the 19th century emphasized author and title; if a title was not felt to be descriptive, key words or inverted titles were sometimes used. However, neither title nor key word can be relied upon to provide consistency. Thus articles on prison inmates may be listed under prisoners, prison inmates, or inmates.

The citations include the volume and page, but not the date. For users of the basic set, which covers almost eighty years, this omission can be frustrating. Students should be alerted to the chronological conspectus at the beginning of the set, which can be used for reference.

Compared with today's indexes, *Poole's* covered a comparatively small number of periodicals, and those chosen, although not usually scholarly in approach, reflected the interests of a university librarian rather than the public library orientation of the *Readers' Guide*. Hence, although a fair number of widely circulated periodicals are included, most of the titles indexed are those that were considered to have a "higher tone" and to be aimed at well-educated readers rather than the mass market. Student researchers will have to be cautioned to exercise care and imagination when using *Poole's*. They will be rewarded.

The reprint edition of *Poole's* is widely available. If your library does not have it, consider recommending it. At $252 it can open up a whole new world to your students. If that is impossible, another library might photocopy key pages for you.

Some Specialized Indexes

Rose Bibliography (Project). *Analytical Guide and Indexes to the* Colored American Magazine, *1909-1960.* 3 vols. Westport, CT: Greenwood Press, 1974.

Rose Bibliography (Project). *Analytical Guide and Indexes to the* Crisis, *1910-1960.* 3 vols. Westport, CT: Greenwood Press, 1975.

Rose Bibliography (Project). *Analytical Guide and Indexes to the* Voice of the Negro, *1904-1907.* Westport, CT: Greenwood Press, 1974.

The three periodicals indexed by this project are available on film.

These indexes were compiled primarily for researchers interested in tracing the movement for social reform and change. Omitted were articles deemed to be straight, factual reporting that did not attempt to give an interpretation or opinion, as well as most articles of less than a half page.

Each set provides an annotated chronological listing of articles, and author, subject, and title indexes. An unusual feature is the inclusion in the annotations of standard codes indicating the intended audience for each article (popular, literary, scholarly), and the author's opinion about the direction of social change (things were better in the past, are better now, will be better in the future).

Guides to 19th-Century Scholarly Periodical Literature

CRIS: Combined Retrospective Index to Journals in History, 1838-1974. 11 vols. Washington, DC: Carrollton Press, 1977.

CRIS: Combined Restrospective Index to Journals in Political Science, 1886-1974. 8 vols. Washington, DC: Carrollton Press, 1977.

CRIS: Combined Retrospective Index to Journals in Sociology, 1895-1974. 6 vols. Washington, DC: Carrollton Press, 1978.

The latter 19th century saw an increasing number of strictly scholarly magazines. Although most of the assignments suggested in this book rely primarily on more popular sources, this set of computer-generated indexes to specialized material would be useful for making comparisons and for tracing changes in scholarly attitudes. Nontraditional in format and appearance, these indexes combine some of the advantages of computer searching with those of traditional printed indexes. Students may have to be taught how to use these.

Periodical Indexes for the Early 20th Century

Readers' Guide to Periodical Literature. New York: H. W. Wilson,
   1900- .

International Index. New York: H. W. Wilson, 1907- .
   The first volume of the *International Index*, covering 1907-1915,
was originally published in 1916 as the *Readers' Guide to Periodical
Literature Supplement.* It indexes seventy-four periodicals that had
been dropped from the *Readers' Guide* for being too specialized.

Psychological Abstracts. Arlington, VA: American Psychological Association, 1927- .

Public Affairs Information Service Bulletin (PAIS). New York: Public
   Affairs Information Service, 1915- .

NEWSPAPER INDEXES

New York Times Index. New York: *New York Times*, 1851- .
   This is the granddaddy of American newspaper indexes. The reprint
edition reproduces the first few years in original handwritten format;
they are worth looking at! Students are guaranteed to be impressed.
   The early years of the *New York Times Index*, like *Poole's*, must
be used with care and imagination, but the effort is well worth the
time required. Students should be cautioned that cumulation and indexing policies vary from year to year. In some years editorial matter
is indexed separately from news articles; some years the news articles
are divided into political, foreign, and miscellaneous categories; some
years have only quarterly cumulations. Terminology and subject headings need to be approached with an open mind. Broad categories such
as art, explosions, or fiction should be consulted as well as narrower
ones such as personal and place names and specific events.
   The *New York Times Index* is widely available. If the early years
are not in your college library, they are probably available in another
library close by.

Personal Name Index to the New York Times Index, *1851-1975.* Suc-
   casunna, NJ: Roxbury Data Interface, 1977; and *Supplement,
   1975-1979; Supplement, 1975-1984.* Verdi, NV: Roxbury Interface, 1984, 1986.
   This index to all personal names that appear in the *New York Times
Index*, in entry annotations as well as in separate entries, enables students to quickly trace a person's life and career (as reported in the

Times). In addition to following a well-known person, students using this set can ascertain quickly whether or not a somewhat obscure person was ever written about in that newspaper. The personal name index must be used in conjunction with the *Times* index, because citations are to the index and not to the *Times* itself. The 1975-84 supplement should always be checked since it includes a significant number of entries omitted from the main set.

Any library that owns the *New York Times Index* for even part of the period covered should consider acquiring this adjunct. It is always classed as a reference book, and complete volumes will not be available through interlibrary loan; however, a cooperative library might be willing to photocopy a limited number of pages.

Indexes to Newspapers of Local Interest

Many newspapers of local interest have been indexed at various times through the years. Although frequently of uneven quality, and with significant gaps in coverage, these indexes are likely to be interesting sources for students in the localities they cover.

Reference librarians at the college usually know what is available locally. The most likely places to look for locally compiled indexes are the local history section of a university library, or the public library or historical society.

Milner, Anita Cheek. *Newspaper Indexes: A Location and Subject Guide for Researchers.* 3 vols. Metuchen, NJ: Scarecrow Press, 1977-82.

This exceedingly useful set contains lists of commercial and noncommercial indexes to a wide range of American newspapers. Among the indexes listed are: all the newspapers of Alabama from 1820 on, in the state Department of Archives and History; the *Nebraska Herald*, 1865-1872, in the Nebraska State Historical Society; the *Brookings Register,* 1890-1977, in the Brookings, South Dakota Public Library, and the *New Mexican,* 1862-1912, in the Museum of New Mexico in Santa Fe.

BROWSING IN NONINDEXED NEWSPAPERS AND MAGAZINES

Although librarians are eager to have students know about and use periodical indexes, many times indexes are not available, or are not the most efficient approach for the subject being considered. In those cases the researcher obviously must go to the periodical directly and browse through it. Although browsing is frowned upon as a method of locating information when more direct methods are available, it is important for students to recognize when it is appropriate and to know how to do it efficiently.

Browsing is appropriate not only when there is no index to the available periodicals or newspapers, but also when the researcher is looking for a very broad picture of an era, when there is a periodical entirely devoted to one subject, or when what is being studied is the periodical itself.

Among the best 19th-century magazines in which students can practice browsing are the very large number of special interest periodicals. These range from magazines written for farmers to those written for children; from the *Lowell Offering* written by and for the shopgirls of Lowell, Massachusetts, to *The Working Man's Advocate*; from *Graham's Journal of Health and Longevity* to the *Art Amateur* to *The Journal of Prison Discipline and Philanthropy*.

Some Approaches to Assignments Based on Browsing

- Read, from cover to cover, five issues of the *New York Times* between 1851 and 1860. Describe everything you can learn about slavery from them.

- Read five copies of any newspaper published from 1890 to 1910. Describe what you learn about public health.

- Read ten issues of a popular magazine. Look for the patterns; what can you learn about politics, economics, education, daily life? What were the important issues and controversies as reflected in these periodicals?

- Look at advertisements in a series of newspapers or magazines for any period; what can you learn about taste, life-styles, products?

- Read five copies of a periodical devoted to art (or music). What seem to have been the most important names? What were the controversies? What was the preferred style? Who wrote the periodical and what can you tell about its readers?

- Read copies of a periodical published by a special interest group (Quakers, Shakers, socialists). What can you learn about the ideas, the life, the habits, the influence of the group?

- Browsing through periodical indexes is valuable in itself, and a good way for students to learn that the same material can be both a secondary and a primary source. Browsing through indexes helps students trace changing interests and discover changing terminology; for example, when did we stop referring to "dangerous classes" and "juvenile depravity?"[2]

Guides to Nonindexed Magazines

American Periodicals, 1741-1900: An Index to the Microfilm Collections. Edited by Jean Hoornstra and Trudy Heath. Ann Arbor, MI: University Microfilms International, 1979.

This is the best guide to American 19th-century periodicals. It describes more than 1,100 periodicals in terms of content, intended audience, size of circulation, and names of important editors and writers. It includes an informative, detailed subject index. Best of all, every title described is available on microfilm as part of the *American Periodicals* series. The guide comes with the microfilm set for those who purchase any part of the set, but has also been purchased separately by many libraries that did not purchase any of the film.

Bullock, Penelope L. *The Afro-American Periodical Press, 1838-1909.* Baton Rouge, LA: Louisiana State University Press, 1981.

This guide contains full descriptions of the content and publishing history of these periodicals. Many of the titles discussed are on microfilm; a selected location guide is provided for all titles.

Appendix C is a selected list of special interest magazines available on microfilm as part of the *American Periodicals* series but not indexed in either *Poole's* or the *Readers' Guide.*

LOCATING THE NEEDED JOURNALS AND NEWSPAPERS

American Periodicals. Series I: 1741-1800, 33 reels; Series II: 1800-1850, 1,966 reels; Series III: 1850-1900, Civil War and Reconstruction, 771 reels. Ann Arbor, MI: University Microfilms International, 1946-1977.

Through this set almost any library can service assignments requiring the use of historical American periodicals. Although extremely expensive in its entirety, individual titles within each series are available for relatively small sums. The complete set, as well as selected titles, is widely available.

U.S. Library of Congress. *Library of Congress Catalogs: Newspapers in Microform.* 1948-1972 cumulation, published 1973; 1973-1977 cumulation, published 1978. Annual supplements thereafter. Washington, DC: Government Printing Office.

This is a world-wide union list of newspapers from all periods that have been microfilmed. The cumulations are dated according to when the holdings were reported to the Library of Congress, not according to when the newspapers themselves were published. The listings are geographical by country, state, and city and include information about publication dates, frequency of publication, mergers, and name changes.

These lists will be particularly helpful to those seeking newspapers published in smaller cities and towns. Included in the lists are many rare and short-lived newspapers, weekly and irregular publications as well as daily ones.

Bound copies of many of these newspapers and magazines are still available. Many of the country's older college libraries, even small ones, still have bound-back runs of some of the more popular magazines, going back into the late 19th century. Historical societies, state libraries, and the older public libraries may have newspapers as well as magazines.

When neither bound copy nor microfilm is available in your library, talk to the librarian about interlibrary loan.

NOTES

1. These criteria were suggested by Kraus, *Murder, Mischief and Mayhem,* pp. 1-4.

2. Shepard, "The Creative Researcher," gives examples of this.

8

Primary Sources: Archives, Annual Reports, Collections, Statistical Sources, and Slave Narratives

This chapter describes a variety of primary sources: archives, annual reports, a clipping file collection, city directories, state census reports, and slave narratives. It is written for those who would not ordinarily use these sources for class assignments, and not especially for historians more accustomed to their use.

A general discussion of each type is followed by a detailed example. These descriptions, which are considerably longer than the annotations to sources appearing elsewhere in this book, will indicate the potential not only of the example described, but of the whole genre. Among a plenitude of suitable sources, I have of necessity made arbitrary choices.

The sources discussed here are the raw materials for the history of almost every discipline in the humanities and social sciences. At least one among them will be appropriate for almost any course in the college curriculum. For each group of sources, there is information on how to identify and locate them.

ARCHIVES

Anyone who has worked with undergraduates knows how difficult it is to convince them that the research process is not mechanical, and that merely reading large amounts of material is useless unless the material is subjected to analysis and thought. Working with an archive can reinforce this concept. It presents students with a challenge of a sort they probably have not encountered before. No one has organized or prearranged the material; no one has guided them toward an expected conclusion. Hence they must think for themselves.

Students being introduced to archival research will find it helpful to understand the difference between the archivist's approach to material and the librarian's. The premises of organization and access are different for each.

Materials in a library are organized according to consistent, standardized rules. These rules enable the librarian to describe both the form and content of each item, and to arrange the materials according to subject. The library catalog reflects these standardized rules and enables users to locate individual items by author, title, or subject.

Materials in an archive are generally kept as collections rather than discrete items, and arranged to reflect as closely as possible the working procedures of the person or organization that generated them. Although many archivists today follow the basic principles of arrangement favored by the Society of American Archivists, archives vary a great deal in the way in which they are organized. Although some archives catalog individual items in the same way as a library does, most catalog only the collections. Many archivists attempt to provide access to individual items within collections by compiling finding aids, which vary greatly in the amount of detail they contain.

Archives on Film

The concept of a completely transportable archive would have amazed an earlier generation. Today, however, geography and fragility are hardly matters for consideration. The use of microform has made collections of archives ranging from *Minutes of Telephone Conversations of John Foster Dulles and of Christian Herter, 1953-1961* (University Publications of America, $690) to *The Papers of the American Fur Company, 1831-1839* (Datamics, $1,335) to the *Correspondence and Records of the Atchison, Topeka and Santa Fe Railroad Company* (Kansas State Historical Society) easily available everywhere.

Although many microform archives are vastly expensive—*The Papers of the American Board of Commissioners for Foreign Missions on Microfilm* (Research Publications) costs $30,400—others are moderately priced. The cost of the *Session Minutes of the Associated Reform Church of Oxford, Ohio, 1839-1849* (Presbyterian Historical

Society), for example, is only $20. Most commercially filmed archives have printed finding aids that simplify their use.

An example of a set that includes both organizational archives and personal papers, and has potential for use in a large number of research projects in many subject areas is:

The Jane Addams Papers. Ann Arbor, MI: University Microfilms International, 1984. Microfilm.
The Jane Addams Papers (printed guide). Ann Arbor, MI: University Microfilms International, 1985.

Included in the eighty-two reels of this set are the personal papers and correspondence of Jane Addams and the archives of Hull House, the settlement house she founded with Ellen Gates Starr in Chicago in 1899. Founded to aid the poor, the immigrants, and the working class of Chicago, Hull House was a pioneer in the social settlement movement. Even a short description of its activities indicates how rich its archives are in potential research projects. Hull House ran social, educational, and cultural programs for children and adults; it sponsored a day-care center, a college extension program, a gymnasium, a restaurant, and a Practical Housekeeping Center. Clubs and organizations ran from the Italo-American Fencing and Athletic Club to the Shakespeare Club and the Nineteenth Ward Improvement Club. Hull House also sponsored research studies, and its archives contain materials related to investigations into factory conditions and child labor (1893-1896), tuberculosis (1900-1908), cocaine (1904-1906), newsboys (1903-1905), midwives (1907-1908), and intelligence and poverty (1933).

Among many files of interest here are those of the Hull House Labor Museum (1900-1935), started as a mode of education for adult workers that would "present history and human progress from the point of view of the laborer." The records contain descriptions of the philosophy of the museum and a list of actual items. The museum was open every Saturday evening and "attracted many who never came to any educational programs" (reel 51, no. 30).

Also on reel 51 (no. 32) are the records of the Mary Crane Nursery and League (1908-1935), which contain material of potential interest to students of early childhood education. Included are financial records, descriptions of physical facilities, goals, activities with children and parents, and teacher training materials.

Those interested in popular support for the arts, or public participation in the arts, will find valuable material on reels 51 and 52, which contain programs and schedules for art exhibitions and theater and music presentations. Included are sheet music, lyrics, a few scripts, and scores and librettos from 1892-1928. The list of theatrical presentations ranges from "The return of Odysseus . . . by Natives of Greece living in Chicago" (complete script in English and Greek is included) to *Arms and the Man* (in 1907), Galsworthy's *The Silver Box* (in 1910), and the plays of Gogol, Yeats, and Shakespeare.

Similar material can be found in:

University Settlement Society of New York City Papers. Wilmington, DE: Scholarly Resources, 1978. Microfilm.

The College Archive

The most available archives, and possibly among the richest ones for undergraduate projects, are the college archives. Where available, these offer the obvious advantage of accessibility and give students the opportunity to handle material in its original form. They also help students recognize the need for preservation procedures for unique materials and demonstrate how an archive is organized.

Many topics can be researched in a college archive. One, which offers many subtopics, is the history of the school (founding and early years; role of women, minorities, and other special groups; changes in the geographic, social, ethnic, or religious backgrounds of students). Another is the history of the area (what it was like when the school was founded; how and why it changed; what the relation of school to town was at various times; what other institutions were in the area). Other choices might be the history of education (how the curriculum has changed through the years; how requirements for entrance and graduation have changed; how the administrative structure and the faculty have changed). In addition, the college archives may contain the private papers of local officials and of people associated with the school, as well as all manner of other miscellaneous collections.

Instructors contemplating using the college archives for undergraduate assignments should talk with the archivist or person in charge of the collection first. The archivist is the person most conversant with the available collections and best able to judge which ones are likely to provide enough useful information for student researchers. If the archivist is accustomed to only the most traditional use of the materials, it may be necessary to spell out in detail the kinds of questions you hope your students will be able to answer. It may also be necessary to work out with the archivist potential problems such as opening hours, since archives frequently have shorter hours than the main library, and service policies, since archives are not open shelf collections. In addition, students may need to be taught how to physically handle delicate or deteriorating materials.

ANNUAL REPORTS

Annual reports are interesting for a variety of reasons. First, they are official reports, and we know who wrote them (wrote in the sense of being responsible) as well as for whom they were written. Second, they are interesting because their bias is generally clear. We know that as official records they won't tell everything about an institution, but rather what administrators want known about it. A special advantage is that, because they deal with institutions and organizations whose functions are familiar to students, they are good sources on which students can practice their critical reading skills.

State Reports on Correction and Punishment, Poverty and Public Welfare, prior to 1930. White Plains, NY: Kraus Microfilm Company, 1973. Microfiche.

The states included in this series are California, Colorado, Georgia, Illinois, Indiana, Massachusetts, New York, North Carolina, Ohio, Pennsylvania, and Texas. Periods covered vary a great deal, but many documents date to the first half of the 19th century. Although the complete set of 2,591 fiche costs over $5,000, fiche for individual states may be purchased separately: California's 102 fiche cost $255, Colorado's thirty-nine fiche cost $97, and Georgia's twenty-five fiche cost $57.

Among the reports included are those from: Colorado State Board of Charities and Corrections, 1891-1918; Colorado State Prison Directors, 1851-1879; Illinois Board of Prison Industries, 1904-1914; Massachusetts Agent for Aiding Discharged Prisoners, 1846-1929; Massachusetts Abstracts of Sheriffs Returns Relating to the Poor, 1837-1863; Massachusetts State Board of Health, Lunacy and Charity, 1879-1886; Pennsylvania Mothers' Assistance Fund, 1917-1929; Texas Bureau of Child and Animal Protection, 1913-1914. Even the titles are instructive!

From the reports of the Superintendent of State Penitentiaries of Texas, we learn that between 1870 and 1874 the following problems were reported: the prison was bankrupt and had to borrow money for salaries since the legislature had voted no money for the year; the women prisoners were exceedingly difficult; the main prison industry, the manufacture of osnaburgs, was no longer profitable (1870); the prison was turned over to lessees and most of the prisoners were still working on the railroad (1871-1872); people were being sent to prison solely because they were crippled or deformed; most prisoners were Negroes and were considered unsuited for any but agricultural labor (1873-1874). In addition to the narrative descriptions of these problems and others, there are frequently charts that include information about prisoners' names, ages, nativity, crimes, marital status, and sentences.

From the 1891 reports of the Indiana State Board of Charities, we learn that as of the meeting of April 7, the state legislature has not yet given its attention to the problems of the "abolition of the perquisite system, the abolition of contract labor of the pupils of the State Benevolent Institutions" or to improving the industrial education of the pupils in those institutions. There is also a complaint that the legislature "wants to destroy the usefulness of the board by fixing such a low salary for the secretary that no competent man could afford to accept the position."

The same group's report on the Reform School for Girls and Women's Prison talks about the need to keep those two functions separate, and about the problems that arise when destitute orphans and those who are dependent through "fault or misfortunes of their parents" mix with those who have been "committed for crime or vice."

Work on the State Board of Charities in Indiana at that time could not have been much fun: the report on hospitals commented on "sundry incidents which occurred . . . and which had been made the subject of severe comment by certain newspapers." It appears that during a brief period of time the body of a recently deceased patient was mutilated by rat bites, an epileptic patient killed another patient, and a few days later the epileptic patient committed suicide by jumping from a window. About two months later a mental patient previously judged close to being cured committed suicide by hanging himself in the hospital basement.

Among the topics suggested by these summaries are: the relationship of institutions to the legislature; political pressure and interference with the institutions; the treatment of epilepsy; racial attitudes; definitions of vice; and attitudes toward the interrelationships between physical illness, mental illness, crime, and dependency. Other questions for student researchers are: Who served on these boards? Were they elected or appointed, and by whom? What were their qualifications? What was the perquisite system? What were the contract labor system and the lessee system? What were osnaburgs?

Since this series provides reports from many states over a critical period of time, there are ample opportunities for comparisons across both time and place. Students of history, sociology, public health, social history, and penology will all find a wealth of material in this series.

Because it is in fiche format rather than roll film, this set is particularly easy for groups of students to use. The fiche reports can obviously be supplemented by similar unfilmed reports that might be available in local libraries and archives.

Annual reports of more recent years are available through:

Urban Documents Microfiche Collection, 1972- . Westport, CT: Greenwood Press.
Index to Current Urban Documents, 1972- . Westport, CT: Greenwood Press.

Subscriptions are available to the entire set or to various parts. Individual fiche are available for $3.75 each, with a minimum of five per order, as well as by subscription to geographical region or subject. Many libraries find it efficient to subscribe to the index and order fiche as needed.

This is an ongoing collection of post-1970 reports by a wide range of municipal government departments and commissions in the United States and Canada. Entries in the *Index* are arranged geographically with a subject index. The inclusion of full subtitles, frequently supplemented by descriptive notes, is often sufficient for a potential user to determine the scope of the document.

Included in the 1985 index are: urban design plans; historic district surveys; labor agreements; arson analyses; budgets; newsletters of a botanic gardens, an arts council, and a wildlife sanctuary; minority group census statistics; reports on environmental designs and architectural plans; and a library acquisition list. These are in addition to the expected reports of municipal agencies such as those for housing, economic development, human services, transportation, and law enforcement.

In addition to annual reports available in microformat, the local historical society, municipal archive, or public library may have reports of local agencies.

COLLECTIONS

Probably the largest and most diverse group of materials available in microformat are collections that have been brought together either by individuals, libraries, or other institutions concerned with the subject, or by commercial publishers.

An example of a coherent collection amassed over a long period, and of potential interest to undergraduates, is:

Tuskegee Institute News Clipping File. Tuskegee, AL: Tuskegee Institute, 1978. Microfilm, 252 reels. Printed guide.

A file of newspaper and magazine clippings about blacks, and events that affected them, was maintained at Tuskegee Institute from the early 20th century until 1966. The total number of newspapers and periodicals from which clippings were taken is estimated at between 300 and 500. These include most of the major national dailies, leading southern dailies, major black newspapers as well as several minor ones, weekly and monthly magazines, and some special interest publications. Although no attempt seems to have been made to clip every black newspaper, there was an attempt to cover all sections of the country. Articles from foreign papers were occasionally included.

The set has three series. Series I, the Main File, is arranged by date and subject. Among the subject headings used were: politics, crime, policemen, Ku Klux Klan, agriculture, newspapers and magazines, segregation, education, killings, racial consciousness, labor, the navy, and colonization. Series II, the Miscellaneous File, includes twenty-nine reels of film. It is subdivided into fifteen sections, including lynching, slavery, Emancipation Proclamation celebrations, theaters and motion pictures, cartoons, and art and artists. Series III is composed of Negro yearbooks, subject classification lists, and complete reel notes for the set.

The section on towns and settlements, reel no. 240 in the Miscellaneous File, covers the period 1911-1966. It contains a great deal of information about "Negro towns," that is, towns established and populated exclusively by Negroes. The tone of these clippings ranges from a sound of wonderment in the headline of an obviously white paper in South Carolina in 1931, "North Carolina Town, Controlled by Negroes, Manages Own Affairs," to the outrage of a black paper in the early forties over the appointment of a white postmistress in an all-Negro town. Although a large number of these stories appeared in the thirties and forties and are largely historical in tone, a considerable number of clippings detail the founding of the towns at the time they were started. These include a 1919 advertisement written to attract home buyers to the city of Independence Heights, Texas, "the only exclusively Negro City in the State."

The Emancipation Proclamation celebrations file, also in Series II, contains surprising riches for students of politics, sociology, and rhetoric, as well as those interested in black history. The file includes many clippings relating to the fiftieth anniversary of the Emancipation Proclamation in 1913. There are detailed stories of political wrangling within the commissions set up to plan observances in New York (where some complained about the "peculiar ideas" of W.E.B. Du Bois) and New Jersey (where the commission of seven men included three blacks) as well as the program for the week's activities in one small town. The town's celebration was divided into "theme days." On ex-slaves day, there was a prize of fifty cents for the "best anecdote of Slavery days told by an ex-slave"; on women's day the 500 women expected to attend would hear a paper on "What the Negro Woman is Doing for her Race and Country" and would compete for fifty cent prizes for the best layer cake and the best loaf of light bread; on the day devoted to the mechanical and professional arts, the men would hear a paper on "Mechanics as an Uplifting Force" and compete for one dollar prizes for the best work by a blacksmith, tinsmith, or brick mason.

Perhaps the best known series in the Tuskegee collection is the lynching file, which makes up most of Series II. Stories in this file tell not only of the horrors of lynching but of the quality of life in the South at the time.

On reel no. 224 is a story clipped from the *New York World* of November 7, 1926—a year in which the Tuskegee Institute documented 29 lynchings. The story tells of the trial of seventeen men accused of having participated in a triple lynching and of the investigation of the crime by the grand jury. It discusses particularly the testimony of one Lucy Mooney, who witnessed the crime. Lucy, eighteen years old at the time this story was written, had been given away by her father when she was ten; put to hard labor by her new "owners," she ran away and married a man of fifty-six. When the man also abused her she again ran away. We learn from the news story that Lucy could not read or write and had never been to school.

STATISTICAL SOURCES: CITY DIRECTORIES AND
CENSUS REPORTS[1]

City Directories

City Directories of the United States. Woodbridge, CT: Research Publications. Segment I, through 1860. Microfiche. Segment II, 1861-
1881. Microfilm. Segment III, 1882-1901. Microfilm. Segment
IV, 1902-1935. Microfilm. Ongoing.

Segment I includes all available directories for the period; later segments include the fifty largest cities and others selected for geographical balance. Fiche or film may be purchased by segment or by individual city or state.

City directories, the telephone books of a period before telephones,
were ubiquitous in mid-nineteenth-century urban America. By 1860
there were eighty American cities with populations greater than 13,000,
and all but seven of them had city directories. The first directories
were those of New York in 1786 and Philadelphia in 1791. By 1854
approximately thirty cities had regularly published directories.

The directory for Binghamton, N.Y., for 1856-1857 typifies many.
It starts with a history of the town followed by a separate history of
each of its churches. The bulk of the directory is composed of an alphabetical list of names of individuals and businesses, with their addresses. House numbers had not yet come to Binghamton, so locations
are designated by "near," "west side of . . .," and so on. Listings for
individuals include occupation and give an interesting insight into jobs
of the day, for example, tollgate keeper, moulder, daguerreian opera-
tor, and canal overseer. A few residents, including two farmers, are
clearly labeled "col'd" (colored). The only women listed are "widow
of . . .". Since these were commercial publications there is considerable advertising, which helps the reader to picture life in Binghamton
as it was then.

A far different city is depicted in the directory for Mobile, Alabama,
in 1839. Much larger than the directory for Binghamton, it lists the
names of officials of government bodies and trade associations and
includes information of an almanac type that helps to characterize
Mobile at the time: a gardener's calendar, a list of landings on the
Alabama River, and several pages of charts giving the gold content
of coins from all over the world. Among abbreviations used in the directory are "fwc," for "free woman of color," "fmc" for "free man
of color," and just "col'd" for colored. There are women as well as

men in the alphabetical list of individuals and businesses, and street addresses include house numbers.

In the directory for Lancaster, Pennsylvania, for 1857 are a classi-fied directory of businesses, an alphabetical directory, and a list of fraternal "clubs" that includes the Odd Fellows, the Odd Ladies, the Temperance, and the "Improved Order of Red Men," two of whose officers are the Sachem and the Keeper of the Wampum.

City directories like these are invaluable primary sources for socio-economic data about the cities and the people who lived in them. Stu-dents working in these sources could be asked to: define the com-munity and its economic base; draw a map of the central part of the town and chart and analyze patterns of housing and business location; estimate the population of various ethnic and age groups; and deter-mine the major religious and social groups. The directories in Segment I might prove particularly useful, since they are smaller than those for later periods and are in fiche format, which can be used easily by groups.

Census Reports

State Censuses. Millwood, NY: KTO Microform, 1976. Microfiche.

This set contains all known state censuses taken between 1790 and 1900. Like the city directories, the census reports can be used to de-duce the socioeconomic life of the period. The amount of information varies; some reports have only a few brief tables, whereas others in-clude long narratives. In almost every instance *what* is counted can be as enlightening as the actual numbers. The Minnesota census for 1865 counted whites, Negroes, mulattoes, Indians, and half-breeds. The Rhode Island census for the same year has a substantial narrative section that evidences great concern about the nativity of Rhode Island citizens and the number and role of the foreign born.

The reports for New York State in 1835 are unusually detailed. They enumerate separately the number of male persons, female per-sons, male persons subject to militia duty, male persons entitled to vote, male persons not naturalized, colored persons not taxed, colored persons taxed, colored voters, and married and unmarried females in various age groups. There are also detailed accounts on the number and circumstances of the deaf and dumb, the blind, idiots, and luna-tics. Under "Circumstances" is information on the number supported by charity, the number of sufficient ability to support themselves, and, for the lunatics, the number confined to jail for offenses or for safe-keeping. All categories of statistics are arranged by county and are given for each town within the county.

Available in the convenient fiche format, these reports could be used to analyze some specific aspect of life in one state in one year, or for comparisons across time or place.

In selecting which reports to use, the following source might be helpful:

U.S. Library of Congress. Census Library Project. *State Censuses: An Annotated Bibliography of Censuses of Population Taken after the Year 1790 by States and Territories of the United States.* Prepared by Henry J. Dubester. New York: B. Franklin, 1969. Reprint of the 1948 edition. (This is sometimes listed under the compiler's name.)

This annotated list was the basis for the microform set. (The microform set, however, includes a number of reports identified after the completion of the list.) The brief annotations include information on how often the censuses were taken, who did the actual enumeration and under what authority, and a summary of what was included in each report.

SLAVE NARRATIVES

For a variety of reasons (quantity, inherent interest, pride, guilt), the "slave narrative" is one of the most easily accessible forms of primary source. For the reluctant reader or researcher, as for others, slave narratives have an immediacy and poignancy lacking in official documents and even in most newspapers and periodicals. At the same time they offer students rich opportunities for critical reading and for learning basic research skills. Beyond their obvious value in giving students a deeper understanding of slavery, they offer insight into social psychology, child psychology, anthropology, rural and urban sociology, folklore, religion, and linguistics.

These narratives take several forms: pure fiction, fictionalized truth, "as told to . . . ," true autobiography, and oral history. Although for many years they were viewed with at best suspicion or at worst disdain, they are today accepted by historians as legitimate sources. For a collection of articles assessing slave narratives as history and as literature, see:

Davis, Charles T., and Henry Louis Gates, Jr., editors. *The Slave's Narrative.* Oxford: Oxford University Press, 1985.

How to Locate Slave Narratives in Your Library

Slave narratives, put together with varying degrees of editorial intervention, were extremely popular during the 19th century. One prominent writer has compared their vogue to that of the Western in the 20th century; the more popular narratives frequently sold in editions of over 10,000. They were particularly widely read in the antebellum period because of their emphasis on religious experiences and moral education, and because their scenes of violence and cruelty could awaken a sense of moral outrage while simultaneously satisfying an appetite for sensationalism. They were reviewed both in the abolitionist press and in many contemporary periodicals of more general interest.[2]

Given the large number of these volumes in circulation in the mid- to late-nineteenth century, it would not be surprising to find original printings in the stacks of many of our older university and public libraries. Policies about the inclusion of this sort of older material in the current library catalog vary a great deal; it's best to check with the reference librarian before making any assumptions.

As slavery gradually ceased to be an issue, these narratives faded from general popularity. However, the general upsurge of interest in Afro-American history in the 1960s created a new generation of readers, with the result that today many reprint editions of the narratives, including a number of useful compilations of short narratives, are readily available.

To locate these in your library's holdings, check under SLAVES—UNITED STATES—BIOGRAPHY, and SLAVES—[Name of state] —BIOGRAPHY in the library catalog.

A useful bibliography for selecting slave narratives to be used is:

Brignano, Russel C. *Black Americans in Autobiography: An Annotated Bibliography of Autobiographies and Autobiographical Books Written since the Civil War.* Revised and expanded edition. Durham, NC: Duke University Press, 1984.

The subtitle of this book is misleading since forty-two of the 668 books annotated were published before the Civil War. The book includes an extremely helpful checklist of autobiographies written before 1865 and reprinted after 1945, plus several indexes that can aid in the selection of materials to be read. There is an "Index of Activities, Experiences, Occupations and Professions," and others to "Organizations," "Locations and institutions," and "First publication years."

The oral recollections of ex-slaves first collected by researchers from Fisk University and Hampton Institute in the late 1920s, and later by researchers working for the WPA, have been collected in:

Rawick, George P., ed. *The American Slave: A Composite Autobio-graphy.* 18 vols. Westport, CT: Greenwood Press, 1972. Supplement, Series I, 12 vols. Westport, CT: Greenwood Press, 1977.

A valuable introduction to these narratives will be found in:

Escott, Paul D. "The Art and Science of Reading WPA Slave Narratives." In *The Slave's Narrative*, edited by Charles T. Davis and Henry Louis Gates, Jr. Oxford: Oxford University Press, 1985.

Structuring Research Projects Based on Slave Narratives

Following are some ideas that might be useful in designing research projects based on slave narratives:

- Take advantage of students' familiarity with fictionalized autobiography and "as told to . . ." tales.

- Students might be asked to try to prove or disprove the authenticity of the narrative based on internal evidence or research into other sources.

- An entire class can be involved in such a project, with different groups assigned to providing documentation for specific sections.

- Using *Poole's*, or by browsing in periodicals and newspapers, students can locate articles that provide additional details, or substantiate specific sections in the narrative: for example, education of free blacks, training of a black-smith (cooper, tailor), superstition, religion, house slave vs. field slave, treatment of runaway slaves.

- Ask students to make a list of unfamiliar words and allusions and check them in appropriate sources.

- Where a place is described, ask students to look for another description of the same place in order to determine the accuracy of description.

- Look at advertisements for runaway slaves. The number of these in available primary sources can be supplemented by the hundreds of transcriptions of such advertisements available in:

Windley, Lathan A. *Runaway Slave Advertisements: A Documentary History from the 1730s to 1790.* 4 vols. Westport, CT: Greenwood Press, 1983.

NOTES

1. A project using a census is described in Monkkonen, "Involving Survey Students in Primary Research"; a project using census reports and city directories is described in McClain and Clegg, "Words, Records, and Beyond: Studying About Local Ethnic Groups Through Primary Sources."

2. Bontemps, *Great Slave Narratives,* p. xvii.

9

Legal Sources

Among the most available—and least used—primary research materials are those shelves and shelves of imposing matched bindings loosely referred to as law books. This chapter discusses ways in which widely available legal resources, particularly those related to federal case law, can be used to enrich and enliven even the simplest undergraduate research papers. The approach suggested here does not focus on legal research procedures as such, but rather on the use of legal sources for social science research.

Of the four components of the American legal system (constitutions, statutes, rules and regulations, and judicial decisions), the judicial decisions—commonly called "case law"—are perhaps the most interesting for student researchers. In our litigious society, these decisions have now extended to every conceivable area of human concern.

Are these sources really appropriate for the average undergraduate? It's hard to speak for all, but many librarians can report on the concentration with which students approach these resources, and their enjoyment and competence once they've received even a brief explanation of how the material is organized. Their enjoyment may well stem from their perception that this is "real" research, as opposed to the type of work they did in high school, and is thus worth the extra time and effort required.

Significant but overdone topics such as abortion, capital punishment, and euthanasia can become new challenges when students go directly to court decisions for opinions and arguments rather than relying on newspaper summaries and popular magazines. Historically interesting topics such as the right to strike and contemporary problems such as brain death and rights of adoptees, as well as seemingly timeless topics centered around the rights of minorities and women, can be fruitfully and effectively researched using these sources.

To do research in legal resources, however, students must understand the relationship between the elements in the legal bibliography and the specific research role each type of source can play. For those unfamiliar with these sources, a very brief explanation follows. For more information, talk to your reference librarian or consult one of the books about legal research listed at the end of this chapter.

REPORTERS

These are the classic law books; they are what you see behind Perry Mason's desk on television. They contain the written decisions of the judges for cases brought up on appeal. Each level of court, state as well as federal, has its own reporter series. They are published chronologically as court sessions end. With a bit of orientation, and some help from a legal dictionary, most students can cope intelligently with decisions concerning the political or social issues they are most likely to be researching. Court decisions, besides introducing students to a primary source of United States law, generally represent good examples of how to describe, analyze, and document an argument.

The most widely available and most influential court decisions are those of the United States Supreme Court. They are available in three editions, which vary somewhat in the ancillary matter included, but contain the complete decisions for every case.

United States Reports. Washington, DC: U.S. Government Printing Office, 1754- .

United States Supreme Court Reports: Lawyers' Edition, 1754-1956, and *United States Supreme Court Reports: Lawyers' Edition.* 2nd series. Rochester, NY: Lawyers' Co-op, 1956- .

Supreme Court Reporter. St. Paul, MN: West, 1882- .

BRIEFS

Supreme Court decisions can be enhanced by reading the legal briefs, supporting documents, and oral arguments used to present the case to the Court. This material for the most important Supreme Court decisions from 1793 on is contained in:

Landmark Briefs and Arguments of the Supreme Court of the United States. Frederick, MD: University Publications of America, 1978- . Available either in microfiche or bound volumes.

DIGESTS

Legal digests function as subject indexes to the reporters. They present brief summaries of each point of law raised in each case; complete decisions are not included. The summaries are arranged alphabetically by subject into sections and subsections. The detailed subject index leads the researcher to relevant sections. Digests are the prime finding tools for research in case law. They are relatively simple to use.

There are two sets of digests to Supreme Court decisions. Each covers decisions from 1754 to date.

U.S. Supreme Court Reports Digest: Lawyers' Edition. Rochester, NY: Lawyers' Co-op, 1969- .
U.S. Supreme Court Digest. St. Paul, MN: West, 1944- .

Digests are also available for the lower federal courts and for most state appellate courts.

LAW REVIEWS

Law reviews are the journals of the legal profession. Relevant articles can be located exactly as they would be in any other subject area—through the use of a periodical index. Both *Current Law Index,* 1980- , and *Index to Legal Periodicals,* 1908- , index law reviews and other law-related periodicals. Both have, in addition to the usual subject headings, case-name indexes that enable the reader to find discussions of specific cases.

Student researchers familiar with the use of periodical indexes will have no trouble with either index; those unfamiliar with such indexes can easily learn to use them by starting with either of these two. Both are available through computerized services as well as in print versions.

ENCYCLOPEDIAS

Legal Encyclopedias

The basic format of a legal encyclopedia is the same as that of a general encyclopedia; articles arranged by subject, with an index directing the researcher to the proper volume and page for the topic in question. However, a legal encyclopedia appears to be more scholarly, with each statement being supported by a footnote citing relevant cases and/or statutes. (There are pages in *Corpus Juris Secundum* that have only three lines of actual text, with the rest footnotes.) The presence of the notes need not distract the undergraduate who has no need for that level of documentation. Most articles are preceded by detailed analytical tables of contents; these should be studied carefully by the student. They function as outlines to the contents of the article and can help the researcher isolate the most relevant sections.

Although legal encyclopedias look quite different from other encyclopedias, the student researcher will use them for familiar purposes: for a general orientation to an unfamiliar topic, or for help in narrowing an overly broad subject.

Corpus Juris Secundum. St. Paul, MN: West, 1957- . Updated by
    pocket parts.
American Jurisprudence, 2d. Rochester, NY: Lawyers' Co-op, 1962- .
    Updated by pocket parts.

These are the two standard legal encyclopedias. Where there is a choice, undergraduates might be more comfortable using *American Jurisprudence, 2d.* because its typography is better, and its policy of citing only the most important cases rather than all the cases (as in *Corpus Juris Secundum*) makes its documentation less overwhelming.

A number of encyclopedias written for the nonlawyer can help orient students to the issues involved in legal research and provide citations to the most significant cases. Among the most useful are:

Guide to American Law—Everyone's Legal Encyclopedia. 12 vols. St.
    Paul, MN: West, 1983-85.

An encyclopedia about the law written for the nonlawyer, this makes an excellent introduction to legal topics for undergraduates. Students should be cautioned always to use the index to this set and to follow through on all entries for the topic, since the articles tend to be short and narrowly focused and since there are no *see also* references connecting related materials. These connections are important, but can only be made through the index.

Encyclopedia of Crime and Justice. 4 vols. New York: Free Press,
    1983.
Encyclopedia of Bioethics. 4 vols. New York: Free Press, 1978.

These two encyclopedias provide excellent introductions to the legal aspects of their subjects. Articles are considerably longer than those in *Guide to American Law*, and many contain historical as well as contemporary information. The range of subjects covered in both encyclopedias is broader than might be expected. Each cites relevant cases.

Encyclopedia of the American Constitution. 4 vols. New York: Macmillan, 1986.

Reference Guide to the United States Supreme Court. New York: Facts on File, 1986.

Both of these encyclopedias cover all aspects of constitutional law and history, including topics such as abortion, freedom of speech, and affirmative action, and provide summaries of landmark cases. The four-volume set obviously covers the topics in considerably more depth, but the index to the Facts on File *Reference Guide* provides useful lists of landmark cases under subject headings.

INTRODUCING LEGAL RESOURCES TO STUDENTS

This chapter offers only the briefest possible introduction to some of the sources appropriate for undergraduate research in legal materials. If students are to benefit from the information in the law collection and not be intimidated by those miles of matched bindings, a librarian should provide a general introduction to the nature of legal bibliography and show students how to use the relevant sources most efficiently.

Such a presentation, besides providing a general orientation, will alert students to some unusual but extremely helpful features of the legal literature, such as pocket parts, case-name indexes, headnotes, and analytical tables of contents. If legal sources are not in the library that undergraduates customarily use, the librarian will also provide guidance in using the graduate library or law library.

As with other research projects, instructors will find it best to offer students a list of recommended topics. Discussing possible topics with the librarian before offering them to students will help to ensure a match between assignments and resources and will alert the library staff to potential needs.

Among topics that might work well are:

- problems of freedom of the press (right of journalists to protect sources, televising of courtroom proceedings, censorship, pornography);
- problems of freedom of speech and assembly (advocating violence, the Communist party, the Ku Klux Klan, the clear and present danger doctrine);

- problems of personal relationships and responsibilities (spousal abuse, euthanasia, rights of adoptees, husbands and wives);
- problems of affirmative action and "reverse discrimination";
- problems of crime and punishment (rights of prisoners, insanity defense, search and seizure, preventive detention);
- historical problems (internment of Japanese-Americans during World War II, right to organize labor unions, right to strike).

Browsing through the list of major articles in the encyclopedias discussed above will yield additional ideas.

STRUCTURING ASSIGNMENTS TO MAKE USE OF LEGAL SOURCES

Assignments in these sources can be structured in a pattern familiar to student researchers: overviews, finding tools, primary sources, and works of analysis.

Suggestions for structuring an assignment either partly or entirely based on legal literature follow.

- Look up the topic in one of the nonlegal encyclopedias; write a summary of the article; list unfamiliar terms and get definitions from the encyclopedia or from a legal dictionary; list the most important cases cited.
- After having read about the topic in a nonlegal encyclopedia, look it up in either *Corpus Juris Secundum* or *American Jurisprudence, 2d.* List additional facts supplied. Compare the two articles.
- Read one of the most important cases identified in the article in a nonlaw encyclopedia. (Attempting to follow up directly on cases cited in the legal encyclopedia articles is not always recommended, since the novice researcher may have difficulty deciding which cases are most important.)
- After identifying cases significant to the topic, locate and read a Supreme Court case in a reporter series. Summarize the case. Compare the full decision with the summaries read previously.
- Use a digest to Supreme Court decisions to locate cases on a topic; from the summaries provided select and read the most relevant (or the oldest, or most recent) case. Since so many contemporary controversies have been considered by the Supreme Court, this procedure can be incorporated into many research topics in the social sciences.
- Use either *Current Law Index* or *Index to Legal Periodicals* to locate an article on a specific topic.
- Use the case-table index in either periodical index to locate an article on the specific case that has been read.

- Read the oral arguments and briefs in *Landmark Briefs* for the case that was read.

- Locate a newspaper article about a specific decision; compare it with the actual decision. This suggestion works for historical topics as well as contemporary ones.

While the use of encyclopedias and specialized periodical indexes will be (or will become) familiar to student researchers, the relationships among the legal publications will be new. However, one of the joys of research in legal sources is the logical pattern between related publications; the constant internal references among the various components of the legal bibliography can make moving from one to another fairly direct.

The publication of legal resources is dominated by two companies: West and Lawyers' Co-op. Each company provides internal links among the various components of their own publications. In libraries where most of these publications are available, these internal references can provide their own structure to the research. West provides these references through its key number system, while Lawyers' Co-op provides Total Client Service Library References.

LEGAL RESEARCH: A SHORT LIST OF HELPFUL BOOKS

The following two books written for nonlawyers might be particularly helpful:

Elias, Stephen. *Legal Research: How to Find and Understand the Law.* Berkeley, CA: Nolog Press, 1982.
Lewis, Alfred J. *Using Law Books.* Dubuque, IA: Kendall/Hunt, 1976.

For fuller discussions of legal research, see:

Cohen, Morris L. *Legal Research in a Nutshell.* 4th ed. St. Paul, MN: West, 1985.
Jacobstein, J. Myron, and Roy M. Mersky. *Fundamentals of Legal Research.* 3d ed. Mineola, NY: Foundation Press, 1985.
Wren, Christopher G., and Jill Robinson Wren. *The Legal Research Manual: A Game Plan for Legal Research and Analysis.* Madison, WI: A. R. Editions, Inc., 1983.

Although written for the law student, the language in this guide is nontechnical, and the many charts will be helpful; the background discussion is unusually clear, with an emphasis on the overall organization of the legal bibliography.

10

Biographical Sources: Biographies, Autobiographies, Journals, Diaries, and Letters

This chapter on the use of biographical research in undergraduate writing assignments includes suggestions for projects involving the famous, the infamous, the not so famous, and the virtually unknown.

ADVANTAGES OF BIOGRAPHICAL RESEARCH

The basic pattern of a life is familiar no matter how unusual the details, which is one reason students frequently do well with biographical assignments. They are accustomed to thinking about people; indeed, if there is one area in which they have had experience looking for hidden meanings, analyzing and comparing statements, and looking for causes, it is the realm of human behavior. Because of that familiarity it is relatively easy to generate research questions about people's lives.

Another advantage of biographical research is that it is relatively simple to structure. There are defined parameters that other projects lack. Once the student has an overview of the life of the person in question, choosing one period or event in that life for more detailed research is a fairly direct procedure.[1]

The average social science or history course emphasizes events, ideas, developments, and theories; individuals tend to be studied only as they relate to the main theme. Since there is rarely time within the curriculum to give attention to the complete life story of even an important person, biographies make good supplementary research projects.

LIVES AS RESEARCH SUBJECTS:
SEVERAL APPROACHES

Almost any aspect of human existence can be illuminated through study of the lives of the people—famous, not so famous, anonymous—who participated. Among the basic approaches possible to biographical research are:

- The study of the life of a well-known person who has made a significant contribution. This is done to achieve a clearer recognition of the forces that formed that person and an understanding of the nature and impact of his or her contribution.

- Little-known people can be studied to illuminate, not a specific contribution, but a class of people, a profession, a particular time or place, a social problem or movement.

- Biographies and autobiographies of the famous and not so famous can also be used to enrich and broaden students' understanding of fictional characters and situations by providing real-life parallels.

- Biographical writings can be used to locate information about specific institutions such as schools and prisons, organizations such as labor unions, political parties, and pressure groups, as well as places, industries, and professions.

Sources for locating biographical writings applicable to these approaches are given at the end of this chapter.

BIOGRAPHICAL STUDY OF FAMOUS PEOPLE

Biographical studies offer considerable flexibility in the amount of research, reading, and writing required. Although the topic is self-defined, students working on projects based on the lives of well-known people may need to concentrate on a specific event, period, or contribution. Such studies lend themselves to assignments done in stages designed to build on previous research. Following are suggested strategies for designing biographical research studies.

- Locate entries of at least two pages in a specified number of biographical or general encyclopedias. Write a summary of the major events in the life of the subject. Note any discrepancies in the articles.

- Based on the encyclopedia articles, compile a list of questions to be answered about that person.

- Submit a working bibliography. Requirements can specify the number of primary sources, scholarly articles, articles in popular magazines and newspapers, and books to be included.

- Read two articles (or chapters from books) describing the same event or development in the person's life, then write a comparison of the two.

- Write a short paper examining a major event, problem, or achievement in the life of the subject. This can be based on primary or secondary sources.

- After reading a biography of the person, locate one or more of the primary sources cited by the biographer. Compare the original document with the way in which it is used in the secondary source. The biography read need not be a full-length study. (This can be an extremely enlightening experience for student researchers, but may require some faculty guidance if the student is not to spend an inordinately long time finding a subject for which both documentary and secondary materials are readily available.)[2]

- If the subject lived in the 19th or 20th century, an event can be researched in newspaper and magazine articles written at the time of its occurrence. Students can first summarize or analyze these articles, then compare them with descriptions of the event in secondary works. This is a simple and effective way to introduce these types of primary sources. See Chapter 7.

- Select a number of people connected in some way, such as members of a presidential cabinet, university presidents, or famous labor leaders; locate entries for them in biographical or general encyclopedias. Compare the people: What did they have in common? What is the most outstanding characteristic of each? Is there an explanation for their common achievement? This short exercise will provide practice in analytical writing and a worthwhile introduction to some key library resources.

- A different way to structure a biographical assignment is to have individual members of the class do the work in a sequential fashion, the first person working on the early years, and succeeding people researching early, middle, and late career developments and contributions. Divisions of the life span will vary with the person, but the lives of most people who have made substantial contributions can be divided into segments manageable for individual research projects.

  The serial approach works best with oral reports and discussion, and would be most useful in subject classes where the study of particular individuals adds to the general educational goals. This approach can be used to demonstrate the incremental nature of information gathering. As the project develops, each oral report should be followed by increasingly analytical questions from the rest of the class, with students receiving copies of each report.

- Another approach to biographical research—one that provides good practice in library skills—is to ask each student to select a person relevant to the course, and write either a short article or obituary about the subject, or compose a letter that such a person might have written. However, the name of the biographee should not be revealed. In the second part of the assignment students exchange letters (or articles) with one another and attempt to find out, using the clues provided, who the person was. (The teacher can check the letters for accuracy before the exchange.)[3]

BIOGRAPHICAL STUDY OF THE NOT SO FAMOUS AND NOT FAMOUS AT ALL

Relatively unknown people are usually studied because they are representative of a group, subject, time, or place rather then for a unique contribution or achievement. The study of prisons can be illuminated by the reading of prisoner autobiographies. The study of industrialization or of women's history is enriched by the journals and diaries of early female factory workers. Any local history course will be enhanced by the letters of early settlers in the region, and virtually all of these categories can provide research subjects in English composition.

This approach to biographical study has a number of advantages. It requires students to practice their research skills but does not require them to do a large amount of reading. In addition, it eliminates problems of narrowing the area of research, which can be troublesome when famous people are the subjects of study. Perhaps most important, the lives of the not so famous, or the not famous at all, more accurately reflect life as it was for everyone and, for this reason, may be more interesting to students than the lives of the rich and famous.

The strategies needed for this type of research are quite different from those needed for the study of well-known people. With a well-known subject one looks for a variety of sources that describe and explain the subject's acts and thoughts; the student researcher's main problem may be to sift and eliminate materials. For research focusing on a relatively unknown person, one obviously starts not with the person's reputation and fame but with the written documents that have been left behind. In a sense the fame of such people lies in the very document that they left. The researcher's problem is to identify and locate that document; to study it intensively, searching for clues to understanding; and then to supplement it with readings in ancillary, nonbiographical sources.

The first task is physically to locate the desired diary, journal, or autobiography once it has been identified. In this connection, there are advantages to selecting works published in journals rather than as books. Books of this type are likely to have been published in small editions, and older writings may well have been discarded by libraries that originally purchased them. That is less often the case with journals. Many libraries that routinely discard books they consider outdated have back runs of periodicals either in hard copy or on microfilm. (The micropublishing industry has, in fact, done an amazingly thorough job of filming old and rare journals; less attention has been devoted to books.)

For a discussion of how to locate books and journals not in your library see Chapter 3.

Following are suggestions for structuring assignments based on biographical writings by or about the not so famous:

- Using one or more of the sources listed at the end of this chapter, ask students to select a diary, journal, or autobiography that relates to a subject of interest to them.

- Have students keep a research log of the steps necessary to locate the item. Their search can introduce them to a number of valuable library tools and procedures: interlibrary loan, computerized networks, union lists, local consortia. Students should try diligently to locate the selected item, but they should be free to change subjects if the task proves too difficult or time-consuming.

Once the document is found, ask students to:

- Read it; summarize it; analyze it; compare its descriptions of occupation, locale, groups, and so on with descriptions in other sources.

- List significant events, both personal and social, that are described.

- Through the use of secondary sources (almanacs, yearbooks, historical dictionaries, timelines), list significant world and national events likely to have affected the individual during the time covered.

- Write a letter to the person; ask questions about this person's private life and feelings, work, the famous people and events of the time, and the world as it was then. This is one way to encourage close reading of the text.

- Using secondary or primary sources, try to answer the questions raised in the letter.

IDENTIFYING THE PEOPLE:
BIBLIOGRAPHIES OF BIOGRAPHIES

The following sources will enable the researcher to identify biographical writings according to a variety of characteristics. Sources are arranged in two groups: general works covering many categories of people, and works covering specific categories of people.

General Works

Arksey, Laura, Nancy Pries, and Marcia Reed. *American Diaries: An Annotated Bibliography of Published American Diaries and Jour-*

nals. Vol. 1, Diaries written from 1492-1844. Vol. 2, Diaries written from 1845-1980. Detroit: Gale Research Company, 1983-1987.

This well-annotated reference work is particularly helpful because it includes less than book-length items and has name, subject and geographic indexes. The subject index in volume 1 includes entries such as legal education, log house plans, plantation management, Jews, and Indians. The name index includes people mentioned in the diaries as well as the authors of the diaries.

Briscoe, Mary Louise. *American Autobiographies, 1945-1980: A Bibliography.* Madison, WI: University of Wisconsin Press, 1982.

A well-annotated listing of over 5,000 autobiographies published in book form. The subject index includes vocations, interests, organizations, locations, and people. Many of the items were actually written before 1945, but are included because they were reprinted after 1945. Supplements and updates the following work by Louis Kaplan.

Kaplan, Louis. *A Bibliography of American Autobiographies.* Madison, WI: University of Wisconsin Press, 1961.

An annotated bibliography of separately published autobiographies published before 1945. The subject index includes occupations, places, and important historical events.

Among the best things about the Kaplan bibliography is that all 781 titles are available on microfiche in:

American Autobiographies: Autobiographies Cited in Louis Kaplan's Bibliography of American Autobiographies. La Crosse, WI: Brookhaven Press, 1974. Microfiche.

The autobiographies are sold in seven series arranged by period. (Series II covers 1851-1900 and costs $990.)

Biographical Books, 1876-1949. New York: Bowker, 1983.
Biographical Books, 1950-1980. New York: Bowker, 1980.

Each of these well-annotated works includes a vocation index and a name/subject index. Broader in scope than either Kaplan or Briscoe, this set includes diaries, journals, books of letters, and chapters in collective biographies as well as separately published biographies and autobiographies. There are over 30,000 names in the two books.

Specific Categories

Addis, Patricia K. *Through a Woman's I: An Annotated Bibliography of American Women's Autobiographical Writings, 1946-1976.* Metuchen, NJ: Scarecrow Press, 1983.

An index to books of over twenty-five pages, including collections of letters. There is a subject index and an index to authors by profession or salient characteristic.

Brignano, Russel C. *Black Americans in Autobiography: An Annotated Bibliography of Autobiographies and Autobiographical Books Written Since the Civil War.* Revised and expanded edition. Durham, NC: Duke University Press, 1984.

Indexed topics include activities, experiences, occupations, professions, organizations, locations, and institutions.

Brumble, H. David. *An Annotated Bibliography of American Indian and Eskimo Autobiographies.* Lincoln: University of Nebraska Press, 1981.

First Person Female American: A Selected and Annotated Bibliography of the Autobiographies of American Women Living After 1950. Carolyn H. Rhodes, editor. Troy, NY: Whitston Publishing Company, 1980.

Suvack, Daniel. *Memoirs of American Prisons: An Annotated Bibliography.* Metuchen, NJ: Scarecrow Press, 1979.

Biographical Dictionaries

Students researching the lives of well-known people will want to use biographical dictionaries. They are described in Chapter 6.

NOTES

1. A helpful discussion of the use of biographical assignments is: Alfors and Loe, "Foremothers and Forefathers: One Way to Preserve and Enhance the Library Research Paper." The article includes a research worksheet useful for student biographical projects.

2. Cassara, "The Student as Detective: An Undergraduate Exercise in Historiographical Research," describes a semester-long project of this type.

3. Shipps, "Working with Historical Evidence: Projects for an Introductory History Course."

11

Visual Sources

Research using pictorial sources can work well for many students. It does not carry the potentially negative connotations of "term paper" or "research paper," while giving experience in using the same or similar research tools needed to locate written sources. And above all, most people *like* to look at pictures. Visual sources discussed in this chapter include photographs, posters, magazine illustrations, cartoons, and advertisements.

Used as the basis for written work, visual sources can be surprisingly useful. Each assignment using these sources can require two different kinds of writing: an analysis in response to the specific assignment, and a physical description of the illustration. The analysis provides the opportunity for organization, logical thinking, and imagination; the description calls for a high level of accuracy and precision.

STRATEGIES FOR INTRODUCING VISUAL SOURCES

Listed below are some questions that might help students approach an unfamiliar type of resource, and some suggestions that might be useful for designing the research project.

- Who is the painter or photographer?
- What was the purpose of the picture?
- What was the intended audience?

- What is the title or caption? Is it self-explanatory? Does it give any insight into the artist's intent or attitude?

- Write a detailed description of the picture: list every object and person; describe each one separately; describe their relationship to each other.

- What details might enable you to date the picture? To locate it geographically? To ascertain the class, occupation, or other facts about the people?

- Analyzing the objects: List and describe any objects with which you are unfamiliar, or that you suspect are being used in an unfamiliar fashion. How can you find out what they are?

- Analyzing people: What can you tell from the dress of the person pictured? The posture? The face? Where is the person looking? Why? What is the relationship between people in the picture? Given what you know about them, is this unusual?

- Analyzing the situation or event: What is happening? What is each person doing? Is more than one thing going on? Is there a main event? What is the relationship of the several events?

- Analyzing the setting: Where is this happening? Is the place real or imaginary? Are the details of the setting important to the situation?

- Hidden meanings: Can you detect any implications in this picture that are not evident from a cursory look?

SELECTING ILLUSTRATIONS

What to Illustrate

In literature classes, students can be asked to prepare an illustrated edition of the novel or story they have read. Illustrations can be drawn from sources contemporaneous with the time the story was written, or contemporaneous with the period written about. Illustrations can come from museums, periodicals and newspapers, pictorial archives, or books of reproductions. To illustrate a story by Henry James students might look at books on architecture, interior design, and fashion published in the late-nineteenth century. To illustrate William Styron's *Sophie's Choice* students could locate pictures of concentration camps in newspapers and magazines. To illustrate Whitman's *Leaves of Grass* students might look for photos and etchings of Brooklyn in 19th-century magazines. Copies of medieval manuscripts on color microfiche or illustrated art books could illuminate the reading of Chaucer.

The assignment might require a physical description of the illustration and an explanation of why it was choosen, how it illustrates the work, and how its inclusion would enhance the text. As a variation, the instructor could provide reproductions of works of fairly well-known artists who were contemporaries of the novelist. The students could then be asked to research biographical and background information about one of the artists, choose one or two pictures they feel would be closest to the spirit and intent of the work being illustrated, and defend their choice.

Alternatively, students can go to local museums and select original works of art to illustrate the poems, stories, and novels they are reading. Greek vase paintings or sculpture would be appropriate illustrations for Homer or Keats, American nineteenth-century paintings for Melville or Twain, period model rooms for Jane Austen or Henry James. Students can document their choices with simple sketches, photographs, or museum postcards. The library research component of such assignments would again concentrate on biographical information and the historical background.

Composition and basic skills classes that do not start with literary works can be asked to research illustrations for topics in newspapers and magazines. Subjects could include depiction of foreign countries, children, women, fashion, transportation, local street scenes, or crime and criminals. Research could be limited to locating the illustrations, or could require locating additional information. Writing could be limited to physical descriptions and appropriate captions, or expanded to include comparisons and analyses.

Social science and history classes can be asked to provide visual documentation for an event, a movement, a period, or a place. Students reading about working conditions after the Civil War can locate pictures of child factory workers, mine disasters, or picket lines. Those studying political history can locate portraits and cartoons of major participants and events; those studying urban history can locate street scenes and cityscapes. Such assignments can stand alone or be combined with more traditional research projects.

See Chapter 5 for a discussion of student-made compilations and "pictorial histories."

How to Locate the Illustrations

Newspapers. Newspapers vary in the number of illustrations they use. The *New York Times*, although never highly illustrated, has noted illustrations in its *Index* since 1932.

Magazines. Magazine illustration first became popular during the Civil War and grew in popularity during the second half of the 19th century. However, both *Poole's Index* and the *Nineteenth Century Readers' Guide* can prove frustrating in the search for magazine illustrations from that period, because few of the most heavily illustrated periodicals were indexed by those publications. (Large numbers of citations to illustrated articles do not appear in the *Readers' Guide* listings until close to the middle of the 20th century.) Despite the limitations of the indexes, however, researchers looking for illustrations of specific events or places or portraits of well-known people might still find it helpful to start with the indexes. On the other hand, those looking for magazine illustrations of a more general nature prior to the mid-twentieth century will find browsing in magazines known to be well illustrated more fruitful.

The following are among the 19th-century magazines most likely to prove useful in a search for illustrations. All are part of the *American Periodicals* series.

The American Magazine of Useful and Entertaining Knowledge. 1834-1837.

The Century, A Popular Quarterly. 1870-1930.

The Cosmopolitan: A Monthly Illustrated Magazine. 1886-1925. After 1892 this became one of the country's leading illustrated magazines.

Emerson's Magazine and Putnam's Monthly. 1854-1858. Many woodcuts.

The Family Magazine, or, Monthly Abstract of General Knowledge. 1833-1840. Its many woodcuts are particularly valuable for scenes of towns, cities, and buildings.

Harper's Bazaar. 1867- . Cartoons, patterns, fashion, interiors.

Judy. 1846-47. Many cartoons and pictures.

Vanity Fair. 1859-1863. A comic weekly that emphasized illustrations and caricatures. Antiabolitionist viewpoint.

(See Appendix C and *American Periodicals 1741-1900: An Index to the Microfilm Collections* for more information.)

Visual Archives. Visual archives, previously available in only a very few locations, are now available in microformat. Although generally acquired by libraries to meet the specialized needs of graduate students and faculty, many of these sources could be used to pique the curiosity and interest of less advanced students, even those in English composition classes. As with manuscripts and archives, the variety, and sometimes the quantity, of pictorial material available can be overwhelming. The faculty member may have to do some prior vetting of these materials in order to keep the student from getting lost in data.

For students doing research in almost any aspect of American history or culture during the Depression and Second World War, among the largest and most interesting resources is:

America 1935-1946: The Photographs of the U.S. Department of Agriculture, Farm Security Administration, and the U.S. Office of War Information, Arranged by Region and by Subject. Alexandria, VA: Chadwyck-Healey, 1980. Microfiche.

In the equivalent of three large shoe boxes are more than 1,500 microfiche containing 87,000 photographs taken between 1935 and 1945, arranged according to six geographic regions, with twelve main subject headings for each. The subjects include: the land, towns and cities, people, homes and living conditions, organized society, medicine and health, work, and war. The printed guide has a subject index and a detailed breakdown of each of the main subject headings; references lead directly from the index to individual fiche in each region.

These photographs can be used to illustrate fiction of the 1930s and 1940s, to contrast and compare with newspaper photographs, to compare with the social realism in the paintings of the period, and to illustrate such diverse subjects as religious and educational practices, agriculture, transportation, and industrial history. Of course they can also be the subject of research and visual analysis in themselves.

Among the fiche illustrating strikes and pickets is FW-125, c-5, captioned "San Francisco Dock Strike, 1925-35(?)," which shows two police officers shooting at an unseen target. The fiche (FW-142 and 143) that document the evacuation of Japanese-Americans at the beginning of the Second World War contain dozens of pictures of the evacuees both before and after arriving at the camps; almost everyone in these pictures is smiling. Anyone accustomed to the graphic presentations of crime and social disorder common in the 1980s might be interested in the five photographs included in the section labeled "Dissipation, Crime, Prostitution, Prohibitionism." Prostitution is illustrated in the Midwest by a discreet picture of a man leaving a house, presumably one of ill repute. Dissipation in the Southwest is illustrated by a man "under the table."

Visual sources of a different kind are in:

United States Documentary Posters from World War II. Washington, DC: Library of Congress, Photoduplication Services, 1978. Microfilm.

Three reels of microfilm contain 1,200 posters, most of which were printed by government agencies. The microfilming was done by the Library of Congress as part of a preservation project and is in black and white.

How does a government encourage sacrifice, hard work, and cooperation from the civilian population during a war being fought thousands of miles away? These posters can help answer that question. They show which issues the government considered vital and give an interesting picture of the problems of the homefront during the war. Above all they demonstrate the kind of visual images thought to be effective. They will be of interest to students of media, art, history, sociology, psychology, and political science.

The human images in these posters are uniform: the Japanese are always leering and buck-toothed, while the Germans are serious, glowering, and sinister. Americans, too, are uniform in appearance in these posters. We are all white, and mostly all blond. On reel 2 there is a poster with the legend "Team Work Builds Confidence; We're all in the same boat—Farmers, Merchants, Laborers, Manufacturers, Professional Men." Those pictured in the boat are all male and all white and are differentiated primarily by their hats.

The slogans on the posters give a sense of the propaganda techniques favored as well as the problems addressed. A random sample: "What you conserve will save a life, or kill a Jap"; "Don't Kill her Daddy with Loose Talk" (picture of sad little girl); "If You Tell Where They're Going, They May Never Get There"; "If You Don't Come to Work You're Working For the Axis"; "Stay on the Job Until Every Murdering Jap is Wiped Out"; "Night Sight Can Mean Life or Death: Eat Carrots and Leafy Green or Yellow Vegetables . . .". The campaign waged against venereal diseases in the armed forces as well as at home is well illustrated and will look familiar to today's student.

Although the posters can stand alone as sources for observation and analysis, they raise questions that students could research in written sources. Possible research projects range from finding simple explanations for posters proclaiming the need for victory gardens, or "Quiet Please, War Worker Sleeping," to the more complex issues of sabotage, race relations, the role of women, the need to increase industrial production and conservation, and the role of propaganda.

Text-Fiche Collections. In addition to large-scale (and expensive) visual archives, there are now increasing numbers of much smaller documentary collections of photographs that combine a small number of fiche with a book. Text-fiche publications differ from the usual picture book in that they are intended as a source of primary information for scholars, rather than just as an attractive publication. Captions, introduction, and explanations are in hard copy, and the documents (that is, the illustrations) are reproduced on fiche.

The two sets described below are examples of the documentary reproduction of photographic collections as primary sources.

Lange, Dorothea. *Farm Security Administration Photographs, 1935-1939*. With writings by Paul S. Taylor. Edited by Howard M. Levin and Katherine Northrup. Glencoe, IL: The Text-Fiche Press, 1980.

One thousand fifty-four photographs are reproduced on seventeen fiche. The text includes the original captions of the photos, a 1935 report on agricultural labor in California, and information on Lange and her work as well as on the Farm Security Administration.'This set is a very small subset of the fiche in the *America 1935-1946* set discussed earlier.

Riis, Jacob A. *The Complete Photographic Work of Jacob A. Riis*. Edited by Robert J. Doherty. Introduction by Ulrich Keller. New York: Macmillan Publishing Company, 1981. Text-fiche edition.

Contains all known prints (632) of Riis's photographs.

EXPLAINING CARTOONS

Cartoons always have been powerful weapons, but in order to understand them one needs to know the context. That need makes them particularly interesting vehicles for student research projects in history and government. The class can be asked first to describe the cartoon and its individual elements, and second to analyze it, explaining the situation pictured, what is being commented on, satirized or criticized, who the people are, whether the setting or objects have meaning, who the audience was for the cartoon, and so on.

The level of research needed to fulfill this assignment may vary greatly according to the skill of the cartoonist, the complexity of the issue, and the amount of background information the student already has. The assignment might work best if the instructor selects the cartoons or at least approves them before the student starts work. Each student might also be asked to locate and submit two or three relevant cartoons from which the instructor will select one for analysis.

A simpler exercise would require the student to locate photographs (or engravings) and also caricatures of the same person, compare them, and explain the caricature.

Published collections of cartoons can be found in the library catalog, and in *Books in Print* under the subject headings: AMERICAN WIT AND HUMOR, PICTORIAL; POLITICAL CARTOONS; and the names of persons, ethnic groups, and topical subjects with the subdivision CARICATURES AND CARTOONS, for example, U.S.–FOREIGN RELATIONS–CARICATURES AND CARTOONS.

One particularly useful book of political cartoons is:

Blaisdell, Thomas C., and Peter Selz. *The American Presidency in Political Cartoons: 1776-1976.* Salt Lake City, UT: Peregrine Smith, Inc., 1976.

For an interesting documentary collection of cartoons, see:

Tuskegee Institute News Clipping File. Series II, Reel 240: "Cartoons, 1901-1946."

(See Chapter 8 for a complete discussion of this file.)

This selected group of cartoons on the general theme of blacks in America offers student researchers an opportunity to study pictorial representation of a single theme over time. Although the meaning of most of the cartoons is fairly easy to deduce, researchers might be encouraged to further identify specific individuals and issues through the use of other sources.

The cartoons in this collection generally cover two periods: 1915-1924, and 1945-1946. Those from the earlier period appear to be drawn largely from the Negro press and illustrate black attitudes toward their own problems and struggles; a few that attempt to picture goals and definitions of progress are particularly interesting. Cartoons from the time of the First World War illustrate the tensions blacks felt in maintaining an attitude of patriotism while continuing to fight for an extension of civil rights. Many of the same themes reappear in clippings from the Second World War.

"READING" ADVERTISEMENTS

The style of advertising copy may well have changed more in the last hundred years than the style of any other form of writing. How did we get from the almost obsequious "beg to inform" and "solicits a call" to today's "Go!" and "Do it NOW!"? The product advertised, the nature of the appeal, and the kinds of products available, as well as the tone of the ads, are social, economic, and technological history at their most vivid, providing almost unlimited options for the research paper.

Among the possible topics that can be described, analyzed, and compared with today's advertising copy are: the depiction of women, children, fathers, mothers, the elderly, and ethnic groups; new technologies; household products; products for personal hygiene and for cure of diseases; and political advertisements. As consumers, students should be familiar with the questions posed by advertisements. Who is being appealed to? What are the inherent assumptions? What is the underlying attitude? What broader problems or conditions of society are reflected by the introduction of the new product or the way in which it is advertised?

Advertisements are located by browsing. Students can be asked to analyze the audience addressed by the newspaper or magazine in addition to describing the content of the advertisements. Interesting comparisons can be made between advertisements in periodicals written for the working classes and those intended for the middle and upper classes.

A Selection of Topics: Headline Events Suitable for Research in Newspapers; Subjects for Biographical Research

HEADLINE EVENTS SUITABLE FOR RESEARCH IN NEWSPAPERS

19th Century

The Molly Maguires, 1862-1877. The violent confrontations of this "secret organization" of coal miners and law enforcement officials ends in a trial.

Civil War draft riots, New York City, 1863. Bloody riots break out between blacks and Irish in competition for jobs; riots are spurred by Civil War draft lottery.

The Great Chicago Fire, 1871.

Philadelphia Centennial Exhibition, 1876.

Jeannette Arctic Expedition, 1879-1882. All are lost in the Arctic seas; three search parties and three years later, story is told.

The Haymarket Square Riot in Chicago, 1886.

Homestead Strike, 1890. An armed battle between Pinkertons and workers kills several during a strike to protest the lowering of wages by the Carnegie Steel Company. This was the bloodiest of the industrial strikes of the 1890s.

World's Columbian Exposition, Chicago, 1892.

The Pullman Railroad Strike, 1894. Wage cuts for railroad workers are followed by boycott, firings, strikes, and violence.

20th Century

The Triangle Shirtwaist Fire, 1911. Tragedy in a sweatshop; many working girls jump to their death from burning building.

The Piltdown Man, 1911. The discovery of a buried skull in 1911 leads to changes in theories of man's early history. The skull was discovered to be a hoax in 1953.

The sinking of the Titanic, 1912.

The Armory Show of Modern Art, 1913. America has its first look at European modern art, and the public is outraged.

The sinking of the Lusitania, 1915.

The Influenza Epidemic, 1918-1919. An estimated 20,000,000 people die in Europe and the Americas.

The Amirstar Massacre, 1919. Indians under British rule crawl through streets; 379 massacred.

The Palmer Raids, 1920. The U.S. attorney general fears a bolshevik revolution in the United States. Thousands of citizens are arrested; many rounded up in midnight raids.

Opening of tomb of Tutankhamen, 1923. Omens and archaeology.

The opening of the Empire State Building, 1931.

The Bonus Army March, 1932.

Olympic Games in Berlin, 1936. Amateur sport confronts Nazi ideology.

Sit-down strikes, 1936-1937. The government estimated that 500,000 workers took part.

Munich exhibition of "Degenerate Art," 1937. The Nazis look at "modern art."

The "Crystal Night" pogroms in Nazi Germany, 1938.

Orson Welles's *War of the Worlds* broadcast, 1938. Thousands believe that the Martians have landed!

The Daughters of the American Revolution and Marian Anderson, 1939. A major patriotic organization refuses to allow a black singer to perform in its hall.

The internment of Japanese-Americans in detention camps, 1942-1945. Japanese-Americans are detained behind barbed wire in "relocation camps" as suspected subversives during World War II.

Dropping of atomic bombs on Japan, 1945.

Centralia Mine Disaster, 1947. One hundred eighteen miners are trapped; dying men leave notes for their families.

The Montgomery Bus Boycott, 1955-1956. Start of a new era?

Murder of Medgar Evers, 1963. A civil-rights activist is murdered in Mississippi. How vigorous was the investigation? How fair was the trial?

SOME INTERESTING SUBJECTS FOR
BIOGRAPHICAL RESEARCH

Probably every librarian has a favorite list of potential biographees; here is mine.

John P. Altgeld, 1847-1902. Governor of Illinois during a period of industrial growth; pardoned the Haymarket rioters; subject of a poem by Vachel Lindsay.

Marian Anderson, 1902- . First black to sing with the Metropolitan Opera—in 1955!

Amelia Bloomer, 1818-1894. Probably the first American woman to wear pants instead of a skirt.

George Washington Carver, 1864-1943. Black American chemist; famous for development of over 300 products from the peanut, the sweet potato, and the soybean.

Charlie Chaplin, 1889-1978. World-famous English actor and comedian was refused reentry to the United States because of his political views.

Mohandas Gandhi, 1869-1948. In 1893 he started fighting against racial segregation in South Africa; later became leader of the Indian people in their fight for independence from England; advocate of passive resistance.

Emma Goldman, 1869-1940. A social radical and anarchist, she was once jailed for urging the unemployed to seize the food they needed. An advocate of birth control and women's rights, she was deported from the United States during the red scare of 1919.

Mary "Mother Jones" Harris, 1830-1930. American labor organizer; protested child labor; led a march of children from Pennsylvania to the Long Island home of President Teddy Roosevelt.

Jack Johnson, 1878-1946. First Negro to win the heavyweight boxing title (1908). Attacked in the press for marrying a white woman. Convicted in 1912 of violating the Mann Act for transporting his soon-to-be wife across state lines.

John L. Lewis, 1880-1969. Possibly the most powerful and certainly one of the most controversial labor leaders of the 20th century.

José Martí, 1853-1894. Cuban poet and essayist. He founded the Cuban Revolutionary Party and was known as the "apostle of Cuban Independence."

Golda Meir, 1898-1979. Former Bronx schoolteacher becomes prime minister of Israel.

Lucretia Mott, 1793-1880. American social reformer and feminist; organized first women's rights convention in 1848.

Jackie Robinson, 1919-1972. First major-league baseball player to break the color line.

Margaret Sanger, 1883-1966. Crusader for birth control; jailed for her activities.

Jim Thorpe, 1888-1953. An American Indian, he was one of the most accomplished all-around athletes in American history; died in poverty.

John Peter Zenger, 1697-1746. American journalist. His acquittal on charges of libel was fundamental in establishing concepts of freedom of the press in the United States.

BIOGRAPHICAL SUBJECTS OF A DIFFERENT KIND

Local heroes: Who were those people who had their statues put in parks and their names given to streets and public buildings?

Appendix B

List of Periodicals Included in the *American Periodicals* Series That Are Indexed in the *Nineteenth Century Readers' Guide*

Arena
Bookman
Catholic World
Century
Critic
Dial
Galaxy
Living Age
New England Magazine
New Englander
New Outlook
North American Review
Outlook
Overland
Political Science Quarterly
Quarterly Journal of Economics
Scientific American
Scribners
Yale Review

Note: Nearly 100 of the periodicals in the *American Periodicals* series are at least partially indexed in *Poole's*. These titles are indicated by an asterisk in the guide to the series.

Appendix C

Selected Special Interest Periodicals

The following is a selected list of special interest periodicals included in the *American Periodicals* series that are not indexed in *Poole's* or the *Nineteenth Century Readers' Guide.* For convenience, series number and reel numbers to the set have been included in this list. Information in the annotations is from *American Periodicals, 1741-1900: An Index to the Microfilm Collections.* This volume, the guide to the *American Periodicals* series, has a detailed subject index, which should be consulted to locate other special interest periodicals.

ART AND ART CRITICISM

Many general interest and "literary" magazines contained articles about art and art criticism and reviews. The following were almost exclusively concerned with art.

The Aldine, the art journal of America. 1868-1879. *APS* III, reels 239-40.

The Magnolia; or Southern Appalachian. A literary magazine and monthly review. 1840-1843. *APS* II, reel 676.

The Art Amateur: a monthly journal devoted to art in the household. 1879-1903. *APS* III, reels 580-85.

Broadway Journal 1845-1846. *APS* II, reel 649.

Includes art criticism.

CRIME AND PRISONS

Journal of Prison Discipline and Philanthropy 1845-1919. *APS* II, reels 480-81 and 1934-35.

The major concern of this journal was prison reform. Annual reports from a number of prisons were regularly included.

Moral Advocate, a monthly publication on war, duelling, capital punishment, and prison discipline. 1821-1824. *APS* II, reel 146

National Police Gazette. 1845- . *APS* II, reels 1318-40.
In the period before the Civil War sensational crime stories were the major feature. From 1866 on sex and scandal became increasingly featured, although some crime stories were still to be found.

Prisoner's Friend: a monthly magazine devoted to criminal reform, philosophy, science, literature, and art. 1848-1861. *APS* II, reels 749-50.

The Remembrancer; or, Debtors prison recorder. 1820. *APS* II, reel 204.
"Concerned with the problem of imprisonment for debt . . . described incidents which occurred in the prisons and listed prisoners received and discharged." It also published poetry and dramatic criticism.

EDUCATION

American Annals of Education. 1826-1839. *APS* II, reels 293-94.
"The first really important American magazine in the field of education . . . it emphasized physical and moral training and advocated education for women."

The District School Journal of the State of New York. 1840-1852. *APS* II, reel 770.
One of the more important education periodicals of the period.

The Common School Journal. 1838-1852. *APS* II, reels 512-14.
Founded by Horace Mann and published in Boston, this important journal aimed at improving the "common" school and education in general. Addressed to parents and children as well as teachers.

FAMILY LIFE

Morality, religion, and family life were extensively treated in many of the general interest magazines. However, some made those topics of major concern.

The Happy Home and Parlor Magazine. 1855-1860. *APS* II, reels 756-57.
"A family-oriented religious magazine . . . [which] did not advocate any particular doctrine and was concerned mainly with improving family life and relations between parents and children and between husbands and wives."

HEALTH AND MEDICINE

A large number of medical journals were available to the profession. The following were written primarily for the general public.

Graham Journal of Health and Longevity. 1837-1839. *APS* II, reel 777.
Nutrition and health; advocated use of "Graham flour."

American Journal of Homeopathy. 1846-1854. *APS* II, reel 365.

"Included discussions of homeopathy and other approaches to medicine, articles describing cures for disease, and accounts of cases in which the homeopathic method was used." Popularly written.

Health. 1845-1914. *APS* II, reels 576-78 and 1692-96.

During the mid-century period, under the title *Water-Cure Journal,* the main concern was with the then very popular practice of using water as a means of curing and preventing disease. In addition, it carried articles dealing with "physiology, pathology, and physical, moral, and intellectual development and gave information on cleanliness, clothing, ventilation, diet, pregnancy and prevention of disease." Later years saw less concern with water cures and a greater variety of articles. Included poetry, recipes, and answers to readers' questions.

The Aesculapian Register. 1824. *APS* II, reel 49.

This bimonthly "published articles on medicine . . . household hints and cautions . . . medical ethics, history of medicine, mental alienation and even vampirism." Included list of deaths and their causes for major American cities, and serious and satirical poetry.

Medical News-Paper. 1822-1824. *APS* II, reel 217.

Opposed quack medicine and the practice of bleeding. Included articles on the state of medicine, and on disease prevention, herbs, and cures.

HUMOR AND SATIRE

Although there were a considerable number of periodicals whose major intent was humor and satire, more were short-lived. The following is a selection from various periods.

Every Body's Album: a humorous collection of tales, quips, quirks, anecdotes, and facetiae. 1836-1837. *APS* II, reel 924.

The   , by Nonius Nondescript. 1826. *APS* II, reel 333.
   Political satire.

The Corrector. By Toby Tickler. 1804. *APS* II, reel 15.
   Political satire.

The Gridiron. 1822-1823. *APS* II, reel 111.

Probably the earliest humorous publication west of the Ohio River. Most of the humor is political satire.

The John-Donkey. 1848. *APS* II, reel 657.

Considered the best of the humorous periodicals of the period. Satire of contemporary events, fads, people, and politics. Each issue contained a political cartoon.

Judy. 1846-1847. *APS* II, reel 481.

A large number of pictures and cartoons.

Puck. 1877-1918. *APS* II, reels 69-84.

"One of the brightest and most original of the 19th century American comic ventures . . . wielded a swift sword against public abuse"; attacked Tammany Hall, the Standard Oil Company, and various presidential contenders. Many political caricatures.

Salamagundi; or, The whim-whams and opinions of Launcelot Langstaff, esq., and others. 1807-1808. *APS* II, reel 44.

"Written by Washington Irving, his brother . . . and his brother-in-law . . . this poked fun at the fads and follies of New York including women's fashions, commented on the theater, and satirized a number of well-known personalities."

Tickler. 1807-1813. *APS* III, reel 45.

Vanity Fair. 1859-1863. *APS* III, reels 568-69.

A well-illustrated satirical weekly critical of the war, abolitionists, and Negroes.

LABOR AND WORKERS

The Lowell Offering. Written, edited and published by female operatives employed in the mills. 1840-1845. *APS* II, reel 675.

A literary magazine, written by the women who worked in the mills, and concerned with their lives and working conditions.

Mechanic Apprentice. 1830-1836. *APS* II, reel 742.

A literary miscellany written and published by members of the Mechanic Apprentices' Association of Boston. Contained fiction and nonfiction.

The Subterranean. 1843-1847. *APS* II, reel 576.

"This magazine was dedicated to the needs of the working man, and proposed to advocate the 'cause of the poor and oppressed,' and fight 'tyranny, injustice and corruption.'" It also contained a considerable amount of poetry, fiction, and miscellaneous material.

The Working Man's Advocate. 1829-1836; 1844-1849. *APS* II, reels 581-83.

An organ of the National Reform Association, this "was one of the more important of the magazines devoted to the interests of the working man." Included foreign and domestic news, poetry, and advertisements.

MUSIC

Many general and "literary" periodicals carried articles about music. The following is a selection of those periodicals devoted largely or exclusively to the subject.

American Musical Journal. 1834-1835. *APS* II, reel 769.

Included vocal and instrumental music, articles about music, and "accounts of the theater, opera, oratorios and concerts in the principal U.S. cities."

Boston Musical Gazette: a semimonthly journal devoted to the science of music. 1838-1839. *APS* II, reel 408.

Included reviews and accounts of musical activities, schools, and societies.

The Euterpeiad: an album of music, poetry & prose. 1830-1831. *APS* II, reel 771.

Devoted almost exclusively to music, included reviews of performances and new and original music.

The Euterpeiad; or, musical intelligencer, and ladies gazette. Devoted to the diffusion of musical information, polite literature, and belle-lettres. 1820-1823. *APS* II, reel 102.

The Monthly Offering. 1840-1842. *APS* II, reel 1245.
A publication devoted to opposing slavery, this included songs with music.

The Musical Visitor, a magazine of musical literature and music. 1871-1897. *APS* II, reels 1289-91.

Printed Music

American Musical Magazine. 1786-1787. *APS* I, reel 6.
Dollar Magazine. A monthly gazette of current literature, music and art. 1841-1842. *APS* II, reel 385.

RELIGIOUS AND ETHNIC GROUPS AND SPECIAL COMMUNITIES

Jews

Israel's Advocate; or, the restoration of the Jews contemplated and urged. 1823-1827. *APS* II, reels 130 and 401.
Devoted to the conversion of Jews to Christianity.

The Jew; being a defence of Judaism against all adversaries, and particularly against the insidious attacks of Israel's advocate. 1823-1825. *APS* II, reel 131.
Devoted to defending Judaism.

Oneida Community

Oneida Circular. A weekly journal of home, science and general intelligence. 1851-1876. *APS* II, reels 670-74.
Discussed the doctrines, beliefs, and activities of the community.

Shakers

The Manifesto. 1871-1899. *APS* III, reels 62-63.
Articles about the Shakers.

Society of Friends

Friends' Review: a religious, literary and miscellaneous journal. 1848- . *APS* II, reels 386-387 and 924-34.

SCIENCE AND TECHNOLOGY

American Reportory of Arts, Sciences, and Manufactures. 1840-1842. *APS* II, reel 646.
Articles on science, manufacturing, and engineering; illustrations, lists of new patents.

Boston Mechanic, and Journal of the Useful Arts and Sciences. 1832-1836. *APS*
     II, reel 472.
     Published by "an association of practical mechanics," this was designed to pro-
vide elementary knowledge.

Scientific American. 1845-   . *APS* II, reels 616-19 and 1734-48.
     Included articles on basic science, manufacturing, technology, and transporta-
tion, with much attention to new inventions. Illustrated. Weekly official patent
list. Circulation by 1850 was 14,000.

SLAVERY, ANTISLAVERY MOVEMENTS

The African Repository. 1825-1892. *APS* II, reels 641-44 and 881-84.
     The official journal of the American Colonization Society.

The Anti-Slavery Examiner. 1836-1845. *APS* II, reel 408.
     Published by the American Anti-Slavery Society, this featured appeals to join
the cause of the society; articles included testimony from slaveholders and material taken from newspapers in the slave states.

The Anti-Slavery Record. 1835-1838. *APS* II, reel 408.
     Also published by the American Anti-Slavery Society, this "was filled with
stories of the suffering of slaves. Almost every issue had a woodcut . . . pointing
out this inequity."

The Cincinnati Weekly Herald and Philanthropist. |1836-1846. *APS* 1409-1412.
Genius of Universal Emancipation. 1821-1839. *APS* II, reels 108 and 1272-73.
     Published from several places including Ohio and Illinois, this magazine favored
gradual abolition and colonization. It included law cases and proceedings of various abolition societies along with the usual articles and poetry.

The Liberator. 1831-1865. *APS* II, reels 391-99.
     Founded and edited by William Lloyd Garrison, this was one of the most fa-
mous and influential of the abolitionist journals.

National Era. 1847-1860. *APS* II, reels 899-903.
     One of the best known of the abolitionist papers, it was the first to publish
(serially) *Uncle Tom's Cabin.* "Its fiery articles did much to incite furor among
the Northern sympathizers."

Vanity Fair. 1859-1863. *APS* III, reels 568-69.
     This comic weekly disapproved of the activities of the abolitionists and had
no sympathy for the Negroes. Many illustrations.

SOCIALISM AND ANARCHISM

The American Socialist. Devoted to the enlargement and perfection of home.
     1876-1879. *APS* III, reel 60.
     The journal of the Onieda group, this contained articles on spiritualism, com-
munism, and free love.

Liberty (not the daughter but the mother of order). 1881-1908. *APS* III, reels
     669-70.
     "A biweekly which for twenty-five years advocated anarchy, free love, and
other radical doctrines." The back page was devoted to poetry.

SPORTS

American Turf Register and Sporting Magazine. 1829-1844. *APS* II, reels 404-7.
     Included shooting, hunting, fishing, and other outdoor sports in addition to
articles about horses.

Forest and Stream. 1873-1930. *APS* III, reels 208-35.
     Hunting, fishing, natural history, and conservation were featured. "Influential
in bringing about conservation reforms."

*Spirit of the Times: a chronicle of the turf, agriculture, field sports, literature and
     the stage.* 1831-1861. *APS* II, reels 620-40.
     "Said to have been the first all-around sporting journal in the U.S." In addi-
tion to racing and sports, it dealt with "agriculture, literature, fashion, and the
theatre; and also published news, court proceedings, poetry, and advertisements."

THEATER

     As with music and art, there was much theater news in general periodicals. A
few short-lived journals made theater a major focus.

*The Dramatic Mirror, and Literary Companion. Devoted to the stage and the fine
     arts.* 1841-1842. *APS* II, reel 605.

The Mirror of Taste and Dramatic Censor. 1810-1811. *APS* II, reel 218.
     "Contained interesting and valuable criticisms of the stage and of theatrical
life." Some issues have a complete play appended.

*The Ramblers' Magazine, and New York theatrical register: for the season of 1809-
     1810.* 1809-1810. *APS* II, reel 43.

*The Thespian Mirror: a periodical comprising a collection of dramatic biography,
     theatrical criticism, . . . "* 1805-1806. *APS* II, reel 44.
     Written by 13-year-old John Howard Payne, later the author of the song "Home
Sweet Home."

WOMEN

     There were dozens of women's periodicals published in this period, most of
them fairly similar in content and tone. Generally included were: poetry, fiction
(mainly of the sentimental variety), music, art, patterns, fashion, and general articles meant to "improve the mind."

*American Ladies Magazine: containing original tales, essays, literary & historical
     sketches, poetry, criticism, music, and a great variety of matter connected*

with many subjects of importance and interest. 1828-1836. *APS* II, reels
420-21.

The favorite cause of the editor and founder, Sarah J. Hale, was female education.

Goodey's Magazine. 1830-1898. *APS* II, reels 772-880.

This was the most popular of the women's magazines. Indexed in *Poole's.*

*Ladies' Garland and Family Wreath, embracing tales, sketches, incidents, history,
poetry, music, etc.* 1837-1850. *APS* II, reels 608-9.

Typical example of a cheap women's periodical of the period.

YOUTH AND CHILDREN

Forrester's Boys' and Girls' Magazine, and Fireside Companion. 1848-1857. *APS*
II, reels 606-7.

A typical children's magazine, this attempted to be both amusing and instructive. It contained stories of adventure and travel, some science, and essays on behavior, along with riddles, puzzles, and poems. Many illustrations.

The Juvenile Magazine. 1811-1813. *APS* II, reel 121.

An unusual magazine, this was intended for Negro children. It was founded
by Arthur Donaldson, who had established a school for blacks in Philadelphia.
Contained information about the school—fees, curriculum, problems—and much
miscellaneous material including instruction in arithmetic, biographies of Negroes,
religious material, and poetry.

Merry's Museum for Boys and Girls. 1841-1872. *APS* II, reels 743 and 1499-1501.

"This very popular children's periodical claimed a circulation of 13,000 in
1852." Contained—in fiction and nonfiction—adventure, morality, instruction,
thrills, natural history, history, and geography. Poems, illustrations, music, and
puzzles included. Edited by Louisa May Alcott from 1867 to 1870.

Appendix D

Sample Research Worksheets

Name: _____

Research Paper Fact Sheet

Working Title of Paper:

1. Period of time encompassed by topic. (Give exact date of first
   story and the year and month of conclusion.)

2. Categories under which topic is indexed.

3. Periodical sources. (List articles in magazines, books, and all
   newspaper editorials on case.)

4. Locale where events took place. (Use an atlas if needed--try to
   find a local map if possible.)

5. People involved. (List major figures in case--victim, killer,
   detectives, etc.)

6. **The amount** of material on my topic is A) enormous B) very great
   C) **adequate** D) somewhat less than adequate E) meager.

Reprinted from Kraus, *Murder, Mischief, and Mayhem,* 134. Permission courtesy of the author.

XAVIER UNIVERSITY LIBRARY

Name _____

LIBRARY EXERCISE

TOPIC _____

I. THE CARD CATALOG

    1. Using the Library of Congress Subject Headings book, find two subject headings which seem to be appropriate to look under in the card catalog.

        _____

        _____

    2. Locate a book in the card catalog under each subject heading and complete the following information for each one:

        Subject heading _____

        Author of book _____

        Title _____

        Publication   Does book have

        Date _____ a bibliography? _____

        Other subject headings under which this book can be located in the card catalog:

        Subject heading _____

        Author of book _____

        Title _____

        Publication   Does book have

        Date _____ a bibliography? _____

        Other subject headings under which this book can be located in the card catalog:

II. PERIODICAL INDEXES

    1. Use a periodical index to find an article on your topic. Complete the following information about the article.

        Name of index _____

        Subject heading used _____

        Author _____

        Title of article _____

Name of journal _____

Journal date _____ Vol. _____ Pages _____

Check the Spindex to see if the Library has the journal _____ Yes _____ No

If the Library receives the journal answer the following:

    What dates does the Library own? _____

    What volume numbers does the Library own? _____

    Is the journal available on microfilm? _____ If so, what years? _____

2. Use another index to find an article on your topic and complete the following information.

    Name of index ____ _____

    Subject heading used _____

    Author of article _____

    Title of article _____

    Name of journal _____

    Journal date _____ Vol. _____ Pages _____

    Does Xavier own the journal? _____ Dates the Library own? _____

    What volume numbers? _____ Available on microfilm? _____

III. ABSTRACTS

1. Use the <u>Psychological Abstracts Thesaurus</u> to find a descriptor for your topic.

    Descriptor _____

2. Use this descriptor to find an article in the <u>Subject Index</u> and complete the following information.

    <u>Subject Index</u> volume number _____ Abstract number _____

    Title of article _____

3. Locate the article in the <u>Abstract Volume</u> and complete the following:

    Author _____

    Journal or publication where complete article can be found _____

    _____

    Institutional affiliation of author _____

Check the Spindex to see if the Library has the journal _____ Yes _____ No

4. Use the Thesaurus of ERIC Terms to find a descriptor for your topic.

   Descriptor _____

   Use this descriptor to locate an article in the RIE Subject Index and complete
   the following information.

   ED number _____ Title of document _____

   Using the ED number, locate document on second floor. Is there a bibliography
   included as part of the document? _____ If so, how many items are in the
   bibliography? _____

5. Using the Descriptor in (4), locate an article in the CIJE Subject Index and
   complete the following information.

   Author _____

   Title of article _____

   Name of journal _____

   Journal date _____ Vol. _____ Pages _____

   Using the EJ number, find the abstract for the article in the Main Entry section
   of CIJE. What descriptors were used to identify this article in the ERIC system?

   _____

IV. LOCATING JOURNALS ON SECOND FLOOR

   Using one of the journal citations you located in section II or III, go to second
   floor and locate the article.

   1. What information is on the spine of the journal?

   2. Scan the article. How closely does the subject content of the article relate to
      the subject heading under which it was indexed?

      Go to the current issue section of second floor and locate the two most current
      issues of the same journal title.

   3. Dates of most current issues:

   4. Scan the table of contents of each of the two most issues. List any article
      dealing with the topic you have been researching in this exercise.

      Title of article _____

      Date of issue _____ Pages _____

Xavier University, Cincinnati, OH.

Name:_____

Your Research Question Is:_____

_____

_____

Develop an annotated bibliography on this topic. It must include
at least one item in each of the categories marked with an X in
the following list. Be aware that the answer to this specific
question has probably never been written down anywhere. If you
were to actually write a paper about it, you would have to decide
on the answer for yourself after studying what has been written
about related problems and about the subject in general. So try
to find a range of material which would help you explore the
topic. There is no upper limit to the length of the bibliography, but since you must read the items to write your annotations, it is unrealistic to attempt more than twelve to fifteen
entries.

Special Note: Some of the items in the list are not ordinarily
included in a bibliography. For example, though you nearly
always need periodical indexes and book-length bibliographies to
develop a bibliography, you should not expect to list them in it.
A similar caution applies to standard reference works. You are
required to list them here only because of the special nature of
the assignment. You might find it helpful to use more than one
of each of these research aids; in that case list the one you
found most helpful. You should expect to have multiple listings
of the other types of sources (No. 4 through 11).

   X 1. One periodical index in your field (not the general
Reader's Guide to Periodical Literature). A list of periodical
indexes is taped to the reference desk.

   X 2. One book-length bibliography. One way to find appropriate books of this type is to use the card catalog subject
index. Their call numbers nearly always begin with Z. You can
find out what subject headings to look under by consulting the
Library of Congress Subject Heading Guides situated next to a
post in the card catalog area. In addition to the card catalog,
you can use this book:

          Sheehy, Eugene P. Guide to Reference Books. 9th ed.
          American Library Association, 1975, and supplements.

   X 3. One standard reference work in your field which you
would expect to consult for any research topic in that field.
For example, in psychology a dictionary of psychological terms

would satisfy this requirement. Many of these works will be
found in the reference collection on the first floor; others
will be shelved in the stacks with other kinds of books on
similar topics. You can find such reference works by following
the recommendations in No. 2 above.

__X__ 4. At least one book with at least a chapter or section in
it that provides information you could use in a paper on your
topic. You may find this kind of book listed in a book-length
bibliography (No. 2 on this list), in the footnotes or bibliography of another book or article, or in the card catalog. To
get the most out of the card catalog, note the tracings, the
various subject headings under which a helpful book is indexed,
shown on the card itself. If you look under all those headings,
you will no doubt find other helpful books.

_____5. At least one article from a major professional journal
in your field. The best way to find articles of this type is
through a specialized periodical index (No. 1 on this list), but
you may also find them through the footnotes or bibliography of
other articles or books.

_____6. At least one article from a weekly or monthly magazine.
You may find these through the Reader's Guide to Periodical
Literature, through PAIS (Public Affiars Information Service), or
in a few cases through a specialized periodical index.

_____7. At least one newspaper article. Check Newsbank or
individual indexes like the New York Times Index.

_____8. At least one ERIC (Educational Resource Information
Center) document. Indexes and documents are housed in the IMC
(Instructional Media Center).

_____9. At least one government document (either United States
or Wisconsin). Indexing systems are in the basement, with the
documents themselves. For some topics, you can also use PAIS to
find government documents.

_____10. At least one sound or video recording or a motion
picture film. The collection of these items is fairly limited in
our library. Though catalogs and indexes for them exist, your
most efficient course is to go directly to the card catalog in
the IMC.

_____11. At least one filmstrip or slide collection. The same
recommendation applies here as in No. 10, above.

_____12. Other:_____

Reprinted from Engeldinger, *Projects Developed for Library Instruction Within the Curriculum*, 57. Permission courtesy of the University of Wisconsin-Eau
Claire.

STARR LIBRARY
MIDDLEBURY COLLEGE
MIDDLEBURY, VERMONT

Name _____   Date _____

NARRATIVE FICTION
FINDING THE LITERATURE: PART II
BOOKS AND JOURNALS

Introduction
    This second part of "Finding the Literature" guides you through an
organized and efficient search for library materials on the topic that you have
defined through the first part. By completing Part II of "Finding the
Literature", you develop a list of information sources pertinent to your topic,
document those search terms that lead to relevant items, and, in the process,
pursue your search as systematically as possible. Part II is due at the next
class session.

    In doing "Finding the Literature: Part II", you will: 1. Restate the topic
as defined in Part I; 2. Identify subject headings that are used in the card
catalog, and that locate books on your topic; 3. Use an appropriate indexing
source for identifying journal articles and list the relevant subject headings
used in it; 4. Choose one relevant publication that you have located, cite it,
and present evidence to use in its evaluation.

1.   Restate Topic
    Restate the focused topic that was developed in "Finding the
Literature: Part I".

    _____

    _____

    _____

2.   Finding Books
    Use the cross reference symbols (sa, xx, x, See) listed in the Library
of Congress Subject Headings, the card catalog, the subject headings listed
at the bottom of catalog cards, or any other technique to select the most
specific, relevant subject headings for identifying books in the library on
your topic. List as many relevant subject headings as are important to
your topic, having first verified that they are used in the card catalog.
Explore all tactics for determining productive subject headings.

    Subject headings:

    _____   _____

    _____   _____

    _____   _____

3.   <u>Finding Journal Articles through Indexing Sources</u>
         Write down the title of the one periodical indexing tool that is the
    best source for identifying journal articles on your topic. Check the
    source, and list the subject headings that lead to relevant citations.
    Note the volume number or date, and page number, of the source in which the
    subject headings were found. Use the General and Multi-Disciplinary
    section of the "Selective Subject Guide to Indexing and Abstracting Tools"
    for suggestions.

    Title of indexing tool: _____

    _____

    Subject headings:

    _____ in vol./date _____ on page _____

    _____ in vol./date _____ on page _____

    _____ in vol./date _____ on page _____

4.   <u>Citing a Publication and Presenting Evidence for Its Evaluation</u>
         Write a correct bibliography citation for a relevant publication that
    you have identified through Part II of "Finding the Literature".   The
    publication should be in the library. Present evidence for its evaluation.
    Such evidence could include the author's reputation, the presence of an
    extensive bibliography, the publication's inclusion in a selective
    bibliography, an evaluative annotation in some source, multiple citations
    in the literature, or other marks of quality.

    Bibliography citation:

    _____

    _____

    Evaluation evidence:

    _____

    _____

    _____

         What style manual did you use to write the citation to the
    publication, found above?

    Name of style manual: _____

    _____

    Permission to reprint courtesy of Terry Plum, Starr Library, Middlebury Col-
lege, VT.

```
Name_____          RESEARCH WORKSHEET
Class_____                            FOR
Library Used_____                   BOOKS
```

Use this section to record subject headings which did not yield any
significant results:

Use this column to record subject headings used in the catalog.	Use this column to record author, title, and publication date of relevant books.	Classification number of book.

John Jay College of Criminal Justice, New York City.

```
Name_____
Class_____
Library Used_____        RESEARCH WORKSHEET
                                       FOR
                                   PERIODICALS
```

Use this section to record indexes and subject headings which did not yield any
significant results:

Use this column to record which   Use this column to record the relevant
Indexes you used; time periods   citations found under each subject heading.
covered; and subject headings
used to locate citations.

INDEX & DATES:
                                         CITATIONS:
    SUBJECT HEADINGS:

INDEX & DATES:
                                         CITATIONS:
    SUBJECT HEADINGS:

INDEX & DATES:
                                         CITATIONS:
    SUBJECT HEADINGS:

Is the periodical Available? If so, Put classification in this column?

John Jay College of Criminal Justice, New York City.

ARTICLE EVALUATION FORM

Author(s):

Title of Article:

Publication Information:

Index or search tool used to locate this article:

On each of the five scales below, rate this article, according to your own opinions, by circling the number at the appropriate point on each scale.

IN MY OPINION, THIS ARTICLE:

was extremely interesting					was incredibly boring
+3	+2	+1	-1	-2	-3

Comments:

was out in left field					was very pertinent to the topic
-3	-2	-1	+1	+2	+3

Comments:

was very easy to understand					was impossible to understand
+3	+2	+1	-1	-2	-3

Comments:

was much too deep or broad			was about right		was too limited or shallow
-2	-1	0	+1	0	-1	-2

Comments:

well-supported and thought out					poorly-supported or over-simplified
+3	+2	+1	-1	-2	-3

Comments:

Reproduced from Engeldinger, *Projects Developed for Library Instruction Within the Curriculum*, 85.

CRITICAL READING ASSESSMENT SHEET

Choose an article on a controversial topic.

I. BIBLIOGRAPHIC DATA:

    A. Title of the Article:

    B. Author:

    C. Name of the publication in which the article appears:

    D. Date, volume, pages:

II. GENERAL SUMMARY

    Here we want to identify and describe:

    (1) the topic of the article:

    (2) the author's position on the issue:

III. THE EVIDENCE

    Here we want to determine and list the specific facts, testimony, comparisons/contrasts, statistics, theories etc. which are cited by the writer to support his/her position.

IV. CRITIQUE OF THE EVIDENCE

    Here we want to determine and analyze how well the evidence presented in III proves or substantiates the author's contention.

V. ANALYSIS OF THE MODE OF THINKING EMPLOYED BY THE AUTHOR; IDENTIFICATION OF ANY FALLACIOUS REASONING.

    Here we want to identify the author's mode of thinking. If it was deductive, what was the universal generalization upon which the argument was built? If it was inductive, was it inductive by sample, cause/effect, analogy?

VI. USE OF LANGUAGE.

    Here we want to identify any emotionally charged words. List them and tell how they misled the reader.

This is an adaptation of a form used by Prof. John Donaruma, Department of Communication Skills, John Jay College of Criminal Justice, New York City.

Appendix E

Tips for Easier Grading
of Student Research Papers

These tips are adapted from a series written by Shirley Schnitzer and Patricia Licklider for the weekly newsletter of John Jay College of Criminal Justice.

- Just before collecting a set of papers, ask students to write a brief statement explaining what they tried to do in the paper and what they believe to be the paper's strongest and most successful aspects. These statements will help you to focus your own thoughts about the paper. Moreover, in responding to their comments, you will be giving students valuable feedback on your perception of their writing as compared with their own.

- Many students have had little or no experience revising their writing. They think of revising as correcting spelling and grammar. You can make the final paper easier to read by demonstrating to them how experienced writers revise their work. One way to do this is by bringing to class a piece of your own writing in its first, second, and third revisions.

- When a paper is clearly a failure do not waste your time marking it up. Instead, see the student in a conference where you can discuss the problems and make concrete suggestions for improvement.

- Collaborative work is a useful learning devise which enables students to get additional research and writing practice without additionally taxing the instructor. Groups can divide up the research to be done, discuss the results, have a recorder make a summary, and then have the group revise and correct the summary. The result can be presented either orally or in writing. The instructor has only one presentation to comment upon and the students have had the advantage of each other's work.

- A better paper is always easier to mark. Don't concentrate all your time on reading the final paper. Instead, require students to hand in a draft and spend part of the time you would have allocated to the final paper in reading and commenting on the draft.

- You do not have to read every research/writing assignment yourself. You can invite students to read and comment on each other's work. Such peer criticism can be surprisingly perceptive.

- At least two weeks before the papers are due, review with your class exactly what you want them to accomplish in the assignment. Distribute a written copy of the objectives and go over each item in the list, even if you already did so when the assignment was first given. As you read the papers, keep the list in front of you, and base your responses on how well the papers have met the specified objectives. Commenting on all the papers in response to a common set of criteria is much easier and faster than responding differently to each paper.

Selected Bibliography

(Note: Works discussed in the text are listed in the Index.)

Alfors, Inez Larson, and Mary Hong Loe. "Foremothers and Forefathers: One Way to Preserve and Enhance the Library Research Paper." *Research Strategies* 3(1985): 4-16.

Beers, Susan E. "Use of a Portfolio Writing Assignment in a Course on Developmental Psychology." *Teaching of Psychology* 12(1985): 94-96.

Beyer, Barry K. "Using Writing to Learn in History." *The History Teacher* 13 (1979): 167-78.

Bleifuss, William W. "Introducing the Research Paper Through Literature." *College English* 14(1953): 401-3.

Bloom, Lynn Z. *Strategic Writing.* New York: Random House, 1983.

Bontemps, Arna Wendell. *Great Slave Narratives.* Boston: Beacon Press, 1969.

Campbell, Judy, and Eileen Ewing. "Stepping Through a Mirror: The Historical Narrative Assignment." *College Composition and Communication* 38(1987): 95-97.

Cassara, Ernest. "The Student as Detective: An Undergraduate Exercise in Historiographical Research." *The History Teacher* 18(1985): 581-92.

Clark, Wilma. "Reaching Across the Curriculum with the Documented Term Paper." *The Writing Instructor* 3 (Summer, 1984): 185-91.

Cunningham, Donald. "A Better Start on Term Papers." *Improving College and University Teaching* 23(1975): 220.

Eichhorn, Sara. "Standards for Public Service of Microform Collections." *Microform Review* 13(1984): 103-7.

Eldredge, Frances. "Why the 'Source Theme'?" *College English* 25(1954): 228-31.

Engeldinger, Eugene A., and Barbara A. Stevens. "Library Instruction Within the Curriculum." *College and Research Library News* 45(1984): 593-98.

Engeldinger, Eugene A., and Barbara A. Stevens. *Projects Developed for Library Instruction Within the Curriculum.* Eau Claire, WI: Wisconsin University, 1983. ED244629.

Estus, Charles, Kevin Hickey, John McClymer, and Kenneth Moynihan. *Creating Effective Community History Assignments.* Chicago: Newberry Library, Paper No. 79-4, 1979.

Faber, Evan I. "Alternatives to the Term Paper." In *Increasing the Teaching Role of Academic Libraries,* edited by Thomas G. Kirk. San Francisco: Jossey-Bass, 1984.

Fink, Deborah. "What You Ask For Is What You Get: Some Dos and Don'ts for Assigning Research Projects." *Research Strategies* 4(1986): 91-94.

Ford, James E., Sharla Rees, and David L. Ward. "Research Paper Instruction: A Comprehensive Bibliography of Periodical Sources, 1923-1980." *Bulletin of Bibliography* 39(1982): 84-98.

Ford, James E., and Dennis R. Perry. "Research Paper Instruction in the Undergraduate Writing Program." *College English* 44(1982): 825-31.

Fulwiler, Toby, and Art Young. *Language Connections: Writing and Reading Across the Curriculum.* Urbana, IL: National Council of Teachers of English, 1982.

Griffin, C. W. "Using Writing to Teach Many Disciplines." *Improving College and University Teaching* 31(1983): 121-28.

Huber, Kris, and Patricia Lewis. "Tired of Term Papers? Options for Librarians and Professors." *Research Strategies* 2(1984): 192-99.

Kerr, Elizabeth M. "The Research Paper as a Class Enterprise." *College English* 13(1952): 204-8.

Koedel, R. Craig. *Local History: Folkore or Documented Fact.* Paper presented at Eastern Community College Social Science Association, 1983. ED232956.

Kraus, W. Keith. *Murder, Mischief and Mayhem: A Process for Creative Research Papers.* Urbana, IL: National Council of Teachers of English, 1978.

Larson, R. L. "Research Paper in the Writing Course: A Nonform of Writing." *College English* 44(1982): 811-16.

Lefevre, Karen Burke, and Mary Jane Dickerson. *Until I See What I Say.* Burlington, VT: IDC Publications, 1982.

McCartney, Robert. "The Cumulative Research Paper." *Teaching English in the Two-Year College* 12(1985): 198-202.

McClain, Shirla R., and Ambrose A. Clegg, Jr. "Words, Records, and Beyond: Studying About Local Ethnic Groups Through Primary Sources." *Social Education* 41(1977): 382-88.

McClymer, John F., and Kenneth J. Moynihan. "The Essay Assignment: A Teaching Device." *The History Teacher* 10(1977): 359-71.

MacGregor, John, and Raymond G. Innis. "Integrating Classroom Instruction and Library Research: The Cognitive Functions of Bibliographic Network Structures." *Journal of Higher Education* 48(1977): 17-38.

Madigan, Chris. "Improving Writing Assignments With Communication Theory." *College Composition and Communication* 36(1985): 183-89.

Monkkonen, Eric. "Involving Survey Students in Primary Research." *Improving College and University Teaching* 26(1978): 158-60.

Mott, Frank Luther. *A History of American Magazines.* 5 vols. Cambridge, MA: Harvard University Press, 1930-1968.

Roe, Kathleen. *Teaching With Historical Records.* Albany, NY: State Education Department, State Archives, 1981.

Salmon, Lucy Maynard. *The Newspaper and the Historian.* New York: Oxford University Press, 1923.

Schwegler, Robert A., and Linda K. Shamoon. "The Aims and Process of the Research Paper." *College English* 44(1982): 817-24.

Shepard, Douglas H. "The Creative Researcher." *RQ* 10(1970): 9-14.

Shipps, Jan. "Working with Historical Evidence: Projects for an Introductory History Course." *The History Teacher* 9(1976): 359-77.

Spatt, Brenda. *Writing From Sources.* New York: St. Martin's Press, 1983.

Stevens, Barbara, and Eugene A. Engeldinger. *Library Instruction Within the Curriculum—The Sciences, Business and Nursing.* Eau Claire, WI: Wisconsin University, 1984. ED266789.

Strickland, James. "The Research Paper Sequence: What to Do Before the Term Paper." *College Composition and Communication* 37(1986): 233-36.

Taft, William H. *Newspapers as Tools for Historians.* Columbia, MO: Lucas Brothers Publishers, 1970.

True, Marshall, and Mark A. Stoler. "Teaching the U.S. History Survey Course: A Staff and Skills Approach." *The History Teacher* 16(1982): 19-33.

Trzyna, Thomas. "Approaches to Research Writing: A Review of Handbooks with Some Suggestions." *College Composition and Communication* 34(1983): 202-7.

Walker, J. Samuel. "Teaching the Method of History: A Documentary Exercise." *The History Teacher* 11(1978): 471-82.

Webb, Eugene J., Donald T. Campbell, Richard D. Schwartz, and Lee Sechrest. *Unobtrusive Measures: Nonreactive Research in the Social Sciences.* Chicago: Rand McNally College Publishing Company, 1966.

Author and Title Index

Subject Index

About the Author

MARILYN LUTZKER, Professor in the Library of John Jay College of Criminal Justice in New York City, serves as Deputy Chief Librarian and Head of Reader Services. Long active in the Library Instruction movement, she is the coauthor (with Eleanor Ferrall) of *Criminal Justice Research in Libraries* (Greenwood Press, 1986) and has contributed chapters to *Teaching the Teachers: On the Job Training for Bibliographic Instruction*, and to the Association of College and Research Libraries proceedings *Options for the Eighties* and *Academic Libraries: Myths and Realities*. Her articles have appeared in *The Bookmark* and *Reference Services Review*.